WHO'S
IN INTERNATIONAL
CRICKET

WHO'S WHO IN SPORT SERIES
Edited by David Emery
Published by Queen Anne Press

Spring 1984
WHO'S WHO IN FLAT RACING

Autumn 1984
WHO'S WHO IN FOOTBALL LEAGUE
WHO'S WHO IN RUGBY UNION
WHO'S WHO IN INTERNATIONAL RUGBY LEAGUE

WHO'S WHO
IN INTERNATIONAL
CRICKET

EDITED BY DAVID EMERY

Queen Anne Press
Macdonald & Co
London and Sydney

A QUEEN ANNE PRESS BOOK
© First Editions (Rambletree Limited) 1984
First published in 1984 by
Queen Anne Press, a division of
Macdonald & Co (Publishers) Ltd
Maxwell House
74 Worship Street
London EC2A 2EN

A BPCC plc Company

Cover photograph of Ian Botham by Adrian Murrell/Allsport.

ISBN 0 356 10410 9 (cased)
      0 356 10411 7 (paper)

Typeset by Jigsaw Graphics
Printed and bound in Great Britain by The Pitman Press,
Bath.

Designed, edited and produced by First Editions, Chancery
House, 319 City Road, London EC1V 1LS

Introduction

Test cricket has been played since 1877, when a match between Melbourne and Sydney XI and James Lillywhite's touring professionals was billed 'Australia v England' it has survived crises such as the Bodyline Controversy of 1933, Kerry Packer's challenge to the establishment in 1977, and the political fighting over the current exclusion of South Africa.

From W. G. Grace onwards, the international game has been illuminated by its supreme exponents and its colourful characters. Modern cricket is lucky. Stars such as Viv Richards, Clive Lloyd, Ian Botham, Bob Willis, Greg Chappell, Dennis Lillee, Rodney Marsh, Imran Khan, Sunil Gavaskar, Kapil Dev and Richard Hadlee stand comparison with the greats of any era.

Who's Who in International Cricket is a unique guide, with career highlights and profiles of current players who have appeared in Test matches for England, Australia, South Africa (before they were exiled in 1970), West Indies, New Zealand, India, Pakistan and Sri Lanka (who played their first official Tests in 1982). Also included are top players from Zimbabwe, who made an impact on the 1983 World Cup. All records are up to January 6, 1984.

Some players' representative honours include both 'Rhodesia' and 'Zimbabwe'. This is of course, the same country but 'Rhodesia' indicates that a player appeared in the South African Currie Cup before the country withdrew from that competition on its independence in 1980.

Abdul Qadir

Born: September 15, 1955, Lahore, Pakistan.
Height: 5ft 7in.   *Weight:* 10st 7lb.
Right-arm leg-spin bowler.
Teams: Habib Bank and Pakistan.

Career Highlights
1978: Took six for 44 to bowl England out for only 191 in his second Test at Hyderabad.
1982: Took seven for 142 off 50 overs to beat Australians at Faisalabad.
First bowler to take 100 wickets in a Pakistan season, 1982-83.

The very name Abdul Qadir conjures up mystery ... and so it has proved even for some of the best batsman since his re-emergence at international level in England in 1982. He took 10 wickets in that three-match series, but the statistics told only half the story. All England's batsmen had to be wary of him and Abdul's googly made some of them look batting novices. Later that year, the Australians went to Pakistan and Abdul was their main tormentor as they lost a short series 3-0.

He missed the 1983 tour to India after a disagreement with the Pakistan Board, who turned down his request for a loan to build a house. The Board issued Abdul a warning that he must *'keep the interests of cricket above his own.'* All was patched up and Abdul joined the 1983-84 return tour to Australia.

Abdul Qadir

Terry Alderman

Born: June 12, 1956, Perth, Western
Australia, Australia.
Height: 6ft 2½in.   *Weight:* 13st 7lb.
Right-arm fast medium bowler.
Teams: Western Australia and
Australia.

Career Highlights
1981: Nine wickets on Test debut, *v*
England, Nottingham, going on to
take 42 in series.

Terry Alderman had to work long and
hard for a regular place in the strong
Western Australia state team, after
making his debut as an 18-year-old. He
was in and out of the side for the next
six years, then a good season in 1980-
81, with 32 Sheffield Shield wickets,
earned him a place on the tour to
England.

He made a sensational start to his
Test career at Nottingham and with
returns like his six for 135 in the third
match of the series at Leeds he set a
record for an Australian in England of
42 victims in the series. No doubt his
spell with Watsonians in Edinburgh
the   previous   year   helped   him
appreciate British conditions.

Alderman, a primary school teacher
whose father was an Aussie Rules
centre-half back, began the 1981-82
season in devastating form and his
match figures of 14 for 88 against New
South Wales in the Sheffield Shield
were the best ever by a Western Australian bowler.

He was a regular member of the
Aussie Test team against Pakistan,
West Indies and New Zealand. But
tragedy struck in his 16th Test, by
which time he had collected 66 wickets. In the first match of the 1982-83
series against England at Perth he
'tackled' a spectator who had run on
to the pitch, dislocating his shoulder

and damaging nerves. He was forced to
reject an offer to play county cricket
with Worcestershire and the injury put
a question mark against his future in
the game.

Terry Alderman

Paul Allott

Paul Allott

Born: September 14, 1956,
  Altrincham, Cheshire, England.
Height: 6ft 4in.   *Weight:* 14st 0lb.
Right-arm fast medium bowler and
  right-handed batsman.
Teams: Lancashire and England.

Career Highlights
1981: Took 85 wickets in English
  season.
1982: Shared record 10th wicket stand
  for England *v* India, putting on 70
  with Bob Willis at Lords.

Paul Allott, a former Durham University student, emerged with Lancashire in 1981, the season in which he returned his career best – eight for 48 against Northamptonshire. He figured in England's stirring Ashes triumph against Australia that season, making his debut at Old Trafford and, as a number 10 batsman, scoring an unbeaten 52.

Injuries have hampered his progress in the past couple of seasons, although he appeared in all of England's World Cup matches in 1983.

Mohinder Amarnath

Born: September 24, 1950, Patiala,
  India.
Height: 5ft 11in.   *Weight:* 11st 9lb.
Right-handed batsman, right-arm
  medium-paced bowler.
Teams: Punjab, Delhi and India.

Career Highlights
1981-82: Captained Delhi to incredible
  success in final of Ranji Trophy,
  when he scored 185 to help his side
  overhaul Karnataka's first innings
  705.
1983: Man of the Match in India's
  sensational World Cup final victory
  over West Indies at Lord's.

Mohinder's achievement in the 1983 World Cup final (he took three for 12 and made 26 in a low-scoring match) climaxed a fantastic six months' run of success which had begun the previous December. In successive series against Pakistan and West Indies he totalled 1,182 runs, with five centuries.

The son of Lala Amarnath, who played 24 times for India, Mohinder made his Test debut as a 19-year-old against Australia, when he opened the bowling. He did not play again until 1976, when he appeared with his brother, Surinder, *v* New Zealand.

He contributed to a famous victory at Port of Spain in 1976 when India scored 406 for four in the fourth innings to beat West Indies, Mohinder making 85.

Amarnath suffered a serious head injury in England in 1979, when he was hit by a delivery from Richard Hadlee, but his confidence was restored by the use of a helmet.

He scored 1,000 runs from Crompton in the Central Lancashire League, 1982, which was a prelude to a rampaging overseas season, when he took his Test career total past 2,500.

Mohinder Amarnath

Dennis Amiss

Born: April 7, 1943, Birmingham, West
  Midlands, England.
Height: 5ft 11in.   *Weight:* 13st 0lb.
Right-handed batsman.
Teams: Warwickshire and England.

Career Highlights
1974: Highest Test score of 262 not
  out *v* West Indies, at Kingston,
  Jamaica, in February when he batted
  for nine and a half hours to ensure a
  draw. Made 1,379 Test runs in a
  calendar year and at Lord's shared a
  second wicket stand of 221 with John
  Edrich, a record for England against
  India.
1976: Best season for Warwickshire
  with 2,110 runs at an average of
  65.93.
1978: Scored two centuries in the
  match against Worcestershire.
1981: Scored two centuries in the
  match against Derbyshire.
1983: In July passed M. J. K. Smith's
  career aggregate for Warwickshire of
  27,672 runs, to become county's
  second highest scorer.

The mild-mannered Dennis Amiss has
been one of England's most successful
post-war batsmen. In 50 Tests he
totalled 3,612 runs at an average of
46.30. He did not score a century until
his 22nd innings, then went on to make
ten more.

He was given his first England
chance in 1966 as a middle order batsman. But it was not until Warwickshire
moved him up to open the innings in
1972, and he was chosen in this role for
England, that he established himself.
On the 1972-73 tour he hit centuries in
successive tests against Pakistan,
followed by a 99. The following winter
he mastered the West Indies attack
with 663 runs in the series. He was
fluent against all but the fastest bowl-

ing and was not the only England batsman to be unnerved by the Australian
pace attack in 1974-75, when Lillee got
the better of him.

The introduction of the protective
helmet rescued Amiss's Test career in
1976. He returned to make 203 against
West Indies at the Oval, despite exceptional fast bowling by Michael Holding,
who took 14 wickets in the match.
However, England sacrificed Amiss in
1977 to make way for Boycott's return
and he has not played Test cricket
since. Not surprisingly he went first to
Kerry Packer's World Series and then
with an unofficial England party to
South Africa in 1982, as a result of
which he was banned from Test cricket
for three years.

He has remained a consistent
scorer with Warwickshire, for whom he
made his debut in 1960. By 1983 he
had moved down the order again but

still scored 1,721 runs. He is a front foot batsman with strong forearms. His favourite stroke is a flick between mid-wicket and fine leg.

Bill Athey

Born: September 27, 1957,
Middlesbrough, Cleveland, England.
Height: 5ft 11in.   *Weight:* 12st 0lb.
Right-handed batsman.
Teams: Yorkshire, Gloucestershire and
England.

Career Highlights
1980: Scored 1,123 runs
to earn his Yorkshire
cap and England
debut.

Voted Young Cricketer of the Year.
1982: Scored 134 against Derbyshire.

Bill Athey played three Tests for England in 1980 and 1981, but managed only 17 runs in six innings as a number three batsman. A brilliant out-fielder, he is hoping that a move from Yorkshire to Gloucestershire for 1984 will improve his disappointing form of the past couple of seasons.

Azeem Hafeez

Born: July 29, 1963, Karachi,
Pakistan.
Height: 6ft 2in.   *Weight:* 12st 0lb.
Left-arm fast-medium bowler.
Teams: Allied Bank and Pakistan.

Bill Athey

Faoud Bacchus

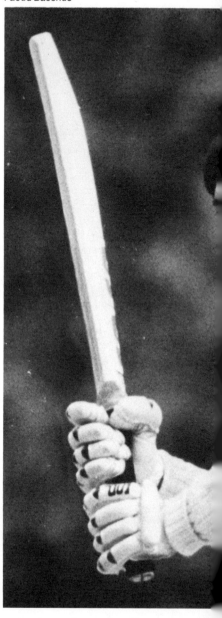

Career Highlights
1983: Took five for 100 against
  Australia at Perth.

Azeem has overcome the handicap of being born with a malformed right hand to play top class cricket. He made his debut against India at Bangalore in 1983, picking up 11 wickets in a three-match series, which was enough to earn him a place on the tour to Australia which followed.

Faoud Bacchus

Born: January 31, 1954, Georgetown,
  Guyana.
Height: 5ft 7in.   *Weight:* 11st 10lb.
Right-handed batsman.
Teams: Guyana and West Indies.

Career Highlights
1979: Career-best 250 when opening
  batting for West Indies against India
  at Kanpur.

Faoud Bacchus made 19 Test appearances without ever being an automatic choice for West Indies, before joining the second rebel tour of South Africa in 1983, when he quickly proved his worth by hitting a century before lunch in a one-day match against Orange Free State.

His double century against India in 1979 included 33 4s and occupied eight and a half hours. He was only six runs short of Rohan Kanhai's best-ever score by a West Indian against India. Faoud topped the West Indies Shell Shield averages in 1982 (326 runs at 81.50) and was again consistent the following year when Guyana won the competition. He played in the 1983 World Cup and was picked to captain Young West Indies in Zimbabwe later that year, but withdrew to go to South Africa.

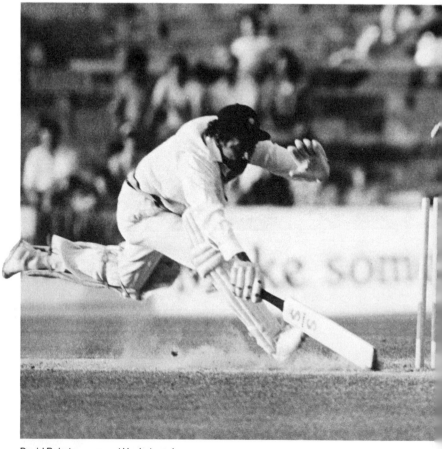

David Bairstow runs out Venkataraghavan

David Bairstow

Born: September 1, 1951, Bradford,
  Yorkshire, England.
Height: 5ft 10in.   *Weight:* 14st 7lb.
Wicket-keeper and right-handed
  batsman.
Teams: Yorkshire, Griqualand West
  and England.

Career Highlights
1979: Made his Test debut against
India and went on to earn four
England caps in two years.
1982: Equalled world record of 11
catches in match for Yorkshire
against Derbyshire at Scarborough.
1983: Scored 1,102 runs to become
first Yorkshire wicket-keeper to top
1,000 runs twice.

David Bairstow is a popular team-man
who, apart from his wicket-keeping, is

made his county debut in 1970 and was appointed captain for 1984 in succession to Ray Illingworth.

Chris Balderstone
Born: November 16, 1940,
Huddersfield, Yorkshire, England.
Height: 6ft 0½in.   *Weight:* 12st 7lb.
Right-handed batsman and slow left-arm bowler.
Teams: Yorkshire, Leicestershire and England.

Career Highlights
1976: Played two Tests for England *v* West Indies.
1981: With David Gower set record second wicket stand for Leicestershire, an unbroken 289 against Essex.
1982: Carried his bat through the Leicestershire innings, scoring 114 out of 246 against Essex at Colchester.

Had Chris Balderstone not followed a dual sporting career, he might well have played more than two Tests for England. As a professional footballer, he appeared in midfield for Huddersfield, Carlisle and Doncaster Rovers. Indeed, on September 15, 1975 he turned out for Leicestershire *v* Derbyshire at Chesterfield, and in the evening played in a League soccer match for Doncaster *v* Brentford.

He has retained his fitness and his appetite for cricket into his forties. Now concentrating on the summer game, he hinted at what might have been by topping his county's batting averages in 1983 with 1,443 runs at an average of 42.44.

an improvising lower-order batsman. He has been invaluable to England in this role on tour.

However, he appears to have missed his chance to take over the England stumper's job from Bob Taylor. Bairstow was dropped in favour of Paul Downton on the 1981 trip to West Indies and has been unable to regain his Test place, despite continuing good form for Yorkshire. He

Eldine Baptiste
Born: March 12, 1960, Liberta,

Eldine Baptiste

Antigua.
Height: 6ft 0in.   *Weight:* 13st 0lb.
Right-handed batsman and fast
  medium bowler.
Teams: Leeward Islands, Kent and
  West Indies.

Career Highlights
1982: Hat trick for Leewards, who beat
  Barbados in final of Geddes Grant/
  Harrison Line limited overs
  tournament.
1983: Earned Kent a place in NatWest
  Trophy final with figures of five for 20
  in semi-final against Hampshire at

Canterbury. Test debut October
1983 *v* India at Kanpur.

Eldine Baptiste followed the Viv
Richards and Andy Roberts trail, from
Antigua to English county cricket,
after being spotted by Kent when they
were on tour. He developed into an all-
rounder to be respected by 1983, his
best season, when he took 50 wickets
as well as scoring two unbeaten centuries (against Sussex and Yorkshire).
He was then chosen to go on tour with
the West Indies to India making his
Test debut at Kanpur and Australia.

Graham Barlow

Born: March 26, 1950, Folkestone,
  Kent, England.
Height: 5ft 10½in.   *Weight:* 12st 12lb.
Left-handed batsman.
Teams: Middlesex and England.

Career Highlights
1981: Shared record first wicket stand
  for Middlesex, unbroken 367 with
  Wilf Slack against Kent at Lord's. Hit
  177 against Lancashire at Southport.

Graham Barlow's England appearances
will be remembered for his scintillating
fielding in the covers or at mid-wicket.
He managed a top Test score of only
five. He has contributed handsomely
to Middlesex's success of the past
decade, and had his best season in
1983 with 1,545 runs.
    Barlow is a qualified PE and
English teacher and has played rugby
union for England at under-23 level.
He began his 1984 season with nearly
10,000 career runs.

Rhaguram Bhat

Born: April 16, 1958, Mangalore,
  India.
Height: 5ft 7in.   *Weight:* 10st 7lb.
Left-arm spin bowler.
Teams: Karnataka and India.

Career Highlights
1982: Performed hat trick and took 13
  wickets in match for Karnataka
  against Bombay in Ranji Trophy
  semi-finals. In final against Delhi
  bowled 94 overs in first innings –
  beating record of 88 overs set by C.S.
  Nayadu in 1945.

Rhaguram made his debut for India at
the age of 25 against Pakistan in 1983.
At least he had a distinguished first
victim – Javed Miandad.

Roger Binny

Born: July 19, 1955, Bangalore, India.
Height: 6ft 0in.   *Weight:* 13st 10lb.
Right-handed batsman, right-arm
  medium-paced bowler.
Teams: Karnataka and India.

Career Highlights
1983: Joint leading wicket-taker in
  World Cup.
1977: Set record (for India) opening
  stand of 451 with Sanjay Desai for
  Karmataka against Kerala at
  Chikmagalur.

Roger Binny, the first Anglo-Indian (he
has Scottish ancestry) and the first
Christian to play for India, was
transformed into a matchwinner during
1983.
    He shocked Australia by taking four
for 29 against them in a World Cup
qualifying match at Chelmsford, thus
assuring India of a place in the semi-
finals. In helping his country eventually
win the Cup, Binny took 18 wickets,
sharing with Asantha De Mel of Sri
Lanka the honour of being the tournament's top bowler. His batting has also
proved useful for India.
    In the 1983 Ranji Trophy final, the
sturdily built Binny showed his
stamina by bowling 43 overs and then
hitting a century for Kanataka against
Bombay.

Stephen Boock

Born: September 20, 1951, Otago,
  New Zealand.
Height: 6ft 1in.   *Weight:* 12st 6lb.
Slow left-arm bowler.
Teams: Otago, Canterbury and New
  Zealand.

Career Highlights
1978: Took five for 67 in his third Test
  match, against England at Auckland.

1977-78: Set a record by taking 66 wickets, beating 57 achieved by George Thompson, member of Lord Hawke's touring team, in 1902/03.

Boock had the thrill of winning his first cap on the occasion of New Zealand's first win over England at Wellington, in 1978. In England that summer he picked up 39 wickets in 13 matches, but has been inconsistent at Test level.

Allan Border

Born: July 27, 1955, Cremorne, Sydney, New South Wales, Australia.
Height: 5 ft 9 in.   *Weight:* 12 st 0 lb.
Left-handed batsman, slow left-arm bowler.
Teams: New South Wales, Queensland, Gloucestershire and Australia.

Career Highlights
1980: Scored 150 not out and 153 against Pakistan at Lahore, to become first player to reach 150 in both innings of a Test match.

Allan Border is the mainstay of the Australian middle order batting, having taken his chance while with New South Wales during the Packer period of 1977-79. He has since moved to Queensland, where he leads the state and is seen as a rival to Kim Hughes for the captaincy of his country.

He served part of his apprenticeship in England, playing for Gloucestershire 2 nds in 1977 (with one first team match against Oxford University) and for East Lancs in the Lancashire League the following season, when he made 1,191 runs and took 54 wickets with his left-arm spinners.

He made a prolific start to his Test career, possessing the style to combat the best bowling and the temperament

Allan Border hits Ian Botham to the boundary

Allan Border

for five-day cricket.

Border piled up 521 runs in the 1979 series against India and 533 against England in 1981, when he showed his bravery by making an unbeaten 123 at Old Trafford while batting with a broken finger.

He passed 3,500 runs during his unbeaten 47 against Sri Lanka at Kandy in 1983 and, despite a disappointing World Cup in England that summer, was back to his best in front of his home crowd with his 10th Test century against Pakistan at Brisbane, maintaining his average of near 50 for Australia.

Ian Botham

Born: November 24, 1955, Haswell,
  Cheshire, England.
Height: 6ft 1in.   *Weight:* 15st 0lb.
Right-handed batsman and fast-
  medium bowler.
Teams: Somerset and England.

Career Highlights

1978: Performed his Test best bowling
  of eight for 34 against Pakistan at
  Lord's. Took hat trick for MCC *v*
  Middlesex.
1979: Reached Test double of 1,000
  runs and 100 wickets in his 21st
  England appearance. Helped
  Somerset win Gillette Cup and
  Sunday League.
1980: Became first player to score a
  century and take 10 wickets in a Test
  v India, in Bombay. Hit 228 *v*
  Gloucestershire at Taunton.
1981: After 42 England matches
  became the youngest player to
  achieve 2,000 runs and 200 wickets
  at 26 years and 7 days (since
  superceded by Kapil Dev). Led the
  amazing England revival against
  Australia, scoring 399 runs, taking 34
  wickets and holding 12 catches in the
  Ashes series in England. Helped
  Somerset win Benson and Hedges
  Cup.
1982: Hit highest Test score of 208 *v*
  India at the Oval. Took a century off
  48 balls for an England XI *v* Central
  Zone at Indore, the fastest 100
  recorded in India. Scored fastest
  century of the English season (52
  minutes) *v* Warwickshire at Taunton.
  Helped Somerset win Benson and
  Hedges Cup.
1983: Hammered 152 (fives sixes, 18
  fours) *v* Leicestershire at Leicester
  while setting Somerset eighth wicket
  record of 172 with Viv Richards.
  Captained Somerset to victory over
  Kent in NatWest Trophy final.

The explosive Ian Botham has been
the dominant player in the England
team since his spectacular debut
against Australia at Nottingham in
1977. His first victim was Australian
captain Greg Chappell and his return
of five for 74 helped England win by
seven wickets. On his fourth appearance, six months later against New
Zealand, Botham hit his first England
century. One of the great all-rounders
had arrived on the international scene,
and his Ashes-winning feats of 1981
prompted from his captain, Mike
Brearley, a comparison with the
immortal W.G. Grace.

Botham, the penetrative swing and
seam bowler, the outrageous batsman,
the stunning slip fielder, dismantled
records like a demolition worker
knocking down mud huts. When his
form has lapsed, he has drawn
criticism from those who judge him
only by his own gargantuan standards.
He has usually answered them when
England have needed him most. In
1981, his century against Australia off
87 balls set up a most improbable
England victory after they had
followed on. For a double encore, he
won the next match with his bowling
and the one after with another century.

His ambitions are to reach the Test
double of 4,000 Test runs and 400 wickets, and to regain the England captaincy he held for 12 matches against
West Indies and Australia from 1980
to 1981 without recording a win. He
leads Somerset full-time in 1984. He
has played League and FA Cup football for Scunthorpe.

He angered Lord's by playing in the
Third Division just 48 hours before
England's 1984 tour of New Zealand –
but proved his fitness by scoring a century and taking five wickets in an
innings (the fifth time he had accomplished this double) in the first Test.

Ian Botham

Geoff Boycott OBE

Born: October 21, 1940, Fitzwilliam, Yorkshire, England.
Height: 5ft 10in.   *Weight:* 11st 7lb.
Right-handed batsman and medium-paced bowler.
Teams: Yorkshire, Northern Transvaal and England.

Career Highlights
1965: Hammered 146 in Gillette Cup final to set up Yorkshire's victory over Surrey.
1970-71: Achieved tour average of 93.86 for England in Australia.
1974: Hit highest score of 261 not out against the President's XI in Bridgetown.
1977: Became first player to score his 100th first class century in a Test match – *v* Australia on his home ground of Leeds.
1982: Shared record tenth wicket stand with Graham Stevenson for Yorkshire of 149 against Warwickshire at Birmingham.

No cricketer has stirred the emotions of supporters, administrators and fellow players more than Geoff Boycott. Since his debut for Yorkshire in 1962, the one-time electricity board civil servant has been obsessed with scoring runs. He achieved what many believed to be his ultimate objective at New Delhi in December 1981, when he overtook Sir Gary Sobers' record Test aggregate of 8,032. Boycott in turn was passed by Indian Sunil Gavaskar two years later.

This dedicated, but self-centred opening batsman developed his talent to its limit after winning his England place against Australia in 1964 and quickly established himself as a player of Test quality. But from quite early on he was accused of disregarding the needs of the team: his highest Test innings – 246 not out in 573 minutes against India in 1967 – resulted in his being dropped by England for slow scoring. Boycott was probably at his peak on the tour to Australia in 1970-71 when, under the captaincy of Ray Illingworth, he played a major part in England's regaining of the Ashes after 12 years. Boycott's haul was 657 runs (average 93.86) in the series.

He chose not to tour India and Pakistan in 1972-73 under a Welsh captain, Tony Lewis; and not to play for England at all between 1974 and 1977 when first a Scot (Mike Denness) and then a South African (Tony Greig) were at the helm. Boycott made a triumphant return in 1977 when England again won the Ashes. He scored 422 runs in three Tests, averaging 147.33. His longed-for chance to lead his country came the following winter when tour captain Mike Brearley was injured. Boycott took over for four Tests, during which England lost to New Zealand for the first time. Brearley was back in charge the following summer.

Boycott's final tour with England was to India in 1981-82. Even his own supporters were dismayed when he returned home early after a controversial incident – while apparently too unwell to field in a Test match, he invited some of his colleagues for a game of golf. Within a short time he was fit enough to join the rebel tour to South Africa and, like 14 others, was banned from Test cricket for three years.

Of the 108 Tests he played, England won 35 and lost 20. Among his 22 Test hundreds (he shares the England record with Wally Hammond and Colin Cowdrey), seven were against Australia and five off West Indies.

He captained Yorkshire from 1971

to 1978, when he was replaced by Jack Hampshire, a change which provoked a bitter feud between the county's pro and anti-Boycott factions. And there was more internal strife five years later when Yorkshire decided not to renew his contract.

He is the only home player to have averaged over 100 in an English season, performing this feat twice in 1971 and 1979. He has scored more runs in Test matches (8,114) than any other batsman apart from India's Sunil Gavaskar. Only Sir Jack Hobbs and Sir Donald Bradman have bettered his 2,945 in England *v* Australia matches.

Geoff Boycott

Brendon Bracewell
Born: September 14, 1959, Auckland, New Zealand.
Height: 5ft 11in.   *Weight:* 12st 0lb.
Right-arm fast bowler.
Teams: Central Districts, Otago and New Zealand.

Career Highlights
1978: Picked to tour England after only three first class matches.

Brendon Bracewell seemed to have a bright future when he toured England as an 18-year-old pace bowler and played in all three Tests, claiming nine wickets. But he has struggled to build on that promising start, partly due to a persistent back injury, and he was not picked when New Zealand next toured England in 1983. He is the younger brother of John Bracewell, who followed him into first class cricket.

John Bracewell
Born: April 15, 1958, Auckland, New Zealand.
Height: 6ft 2in.   *Weight:* 12st 7lb.
Right-arm off-spin bowler, right-handed batsman.
Teams: Otago, Auckland and New Zealand.

Career Highlights
1981: Took five for 75 and nine wickets in match for New Zealand *v* India at Auckland.
1982: Returned seven for nine playing for Otago against Canterbury at Dunedin.
1984: Maiden century (104 not out) Auckland *v* England at Auckland.

John Bracewell made his Test debut against Australia at Brisbane in November 1980 – and joined his younger brother, Brendon, in the team. John played in all four Tests against England in 1983, but his brother was omitted from the tour. Out of season, John has worked as a grave digger!

Ray Bright

Born: July 13, 1954, Australia.
Height: 5ft 11in.　*Weight:* 13st 0lb.
Left-arm spin bowler.
Teams: Victoria and Australia.

Career Highlights
1980: Best bowling of seven for 87 for
　Australia against Pakistan at Karachi.

Bright is a mainly defensive spin bowler used intermittently by Australia since 1977, when he toured England and took 39 wickets. He played World Series cricket between 1977-79 and was appointed captain of Victoria in 1983 in succession to Graham Yallop.

Robin Brown

Born: March 11, 1951, Kadoma,
　Rhodesia.
Height: 6ft 1in.　*Weight:* 11st 6lb.
Right-handed batsman, occasional wicket-keeper.
Teams: Rhodesia and Zimbabwe.

Career Highlights
1978: Maiden first-class century was
　200 not out for Rhodesia B *v* Eastern
　Province B at Harare.

Brown is a farmer who commutes 250 miles every weekend during the season to play for the Old Georgians, in Harare. He was used as an opener during the 1983 World Cup.

Ray Bright

Robin Brown

Ian Butchart

Born: May 9, 1960, Bulawayo,
   Rhodesia.
Height: 6ft 0in.   *Weight:* 11st 11lb.
Right-arm medium-paced bowler,
   right-handed batsman.
Team: Zimbabwe.

Career Highlights
1983: Member of Zimbabwe's World
   Cup squad.

Butchart is an improving all-rounder
who is not afraid to hit the ball hard.
His bowling has been valuable in
limited overs cricket – he twice took
four wickets in an innings against the
Young West Indies team in 1983.

Ian Butchart

Alan Butcher

Alan Butcher

Born: January 7, 1954, Croydon,
    Surrey, England.
Height: 5ft 8in.   *Weight:* 11st 7lb.
Left-handed opening batsman and left-
    arm slow or medium bowler.
Teams: Surrey and England.

Career Highlights
1979: Played once for England against
    India.
1982: Unbeaten 86 helped Surrey to a
    nine wickets win over Warwickshire
in the NatWest Trophy final.

Alan Butcher has a repertoire of
attacking shots. He had his best season
to date in 1980, with 1,713 runs,
including an unbeaten 216 against
Cambridge University. Unfortunately,
he seemed to freeze on his one Test
appearance. Early in his career he
enjoyed success as a bowler, taking six
for 48 against Hampshire at Guildford
in 1972. He was appointed vice-
captain of Surrey in 1982.

Roland Butcher

Born: October 14, 1953, East Point,
St Philip, Barbados.
Height: 5ft 7in.   *Weight:* 12st 0lb.
Right-handed batsman.
Teams: Middlesex, Barbados,
Tasmania and England.

Career Highlights
1980: Spectacular 50 not out at Lord's
in Gillette Cup final helped
Middlesex beat Surrey.
1981: Became first black West Indian
to play for England – and in his
native West Indies.
1982: Hit highest score of 197 against
Yorkshire.

Butcher is a typically swashbuckling
Caribbean batsman, but flaws were
exposed in three Tests for England.
His top score was 32. His adventurous
style has continued to pay off for his
county, however, especially in one-day
games. Roland suffered a setback in
1983 when, hit by a delivery from

Roland Butcher

Leicestershire's George Ferris, a facial injury caused him to miss the second half of the season. A brilliant fielder, he had already taken 37 catches when his season was curtailed. His cousin is Basil Butcher, one of the great West Indies players of the sixties.

Roland is a devout churchgoer and works for Inter-Action in deprived areas of London.

Lance Cairns

Born: October 10, 1949, Picton, New Zealand.
Height: 6ft 1in.   *Weight:* 14st 3lb.
Right-arm swing bowler, right-handed batsman.
Teams: Central Districts, Otago, Northern Districts and New Zealand.

Career Highlights
1980: Hit fastest century recorded in New Zealand – in 52 minutes off 45 balls, playing for Otago against Wellington. Scored 110 out of 170.
1983: Paved way for New Zealand's first victory in a Test match in England with his best figures of seven for 74 at Leeds.

Lance Cairns has toured the world with New Zealand in the past decade and undoubtedly his greatest triumph was against England in 1983, when his bowling proved decisive at Leeds. However, he was brought down to earth in the next game at Lord's, when he dropped three catches, in England's first innings, one of them allowing David Gower to play a match-winning innings of 108. After 32 Tests Cairns had claimed 97 wickets.

Greg Chappell MBE

Born: August 7, 1948, Unley, Adelaide, South Australia, Australia.

Height: 6ft 2in.   *Weight:* 12st 12lb.
Right-handed batsman, right-arm medium-paced bowler.
Teams: South Australia, Queensland, Somerset and Australia.

Career Highlights
1970: Century on Test debut, *v* England at Perth.
1974-75: Scored 608 runs in 1974-75 series against England.
1975-76: 702 runs in series against West Indies.
1982-83: Achieved ambition to captain Australia to an Ashes win with victory in series against England.
1984: Scored 182 for Australia *v* Pakistan at Sydney, making him only player to hit century in first and last Test innings. Also passed Bradman's record of 6,996 runs for an Australian Test cricketer.

Greg Chappell is the most gifted of the modern Australian batsmen and was generally recognised as the best in the world until the emergence of the West Indian, Viv Richards. Greg is a classical, perfectly balanced player with all the attacking shots as well as a straight defence. He is a brilliant slip fielder and a medium-paced bowler able to swing the ball.

His grandfather was Vic Richardson, the Australian Test player of the thirties who captained his country just as two of his grandsons were to.

England's players knew what to expect when they came up against Greg for the first time at Test level at Perth in 1970. The young Chappell had played the 1968 and '69 seasons with Somerset as part of his apprenticeship. He scored 108, going in at No. 7, in his first Test innings and by the time he returned to England with the 1972 Australians he was already a high-class player, getting 131 at Lord's

Greg Chappell

and then at the Oval he and Ian providing the first instance of brothers scoring centuries in the same innings of a Test.

They were to do better than this at Wellington in 1974, when Greg made 247 not out and 133, and Ian 145 and 121. The only other instance of brothers both scoring two centuries in a first class match was R. E. and W. L. Foster for Worcestershire against Hampshire in 1899.

In 1975, Ian handed the Australian captaincy to Greg, who celebrated with 123 and 109 not out at Brisbane and by going on to win a series against the West Indies 5-1. The margin was deceptive, but the fact that Australia were able to overcome a side whose pace bowlers were the scourge of world cricket was in no small way due to the unflinching example of Chappell. Hit in the mouth by Holding, he spat out the blood and took guard again.

He announced his retirement in 1977, to play World Series for Kerry Packer, but he returned, although he has tended to pick his series to suit the business commitments which have made him one of the richest cricketers.

His most fulfilling achievement in the latter part of his career was to win the Ashes against England in 1982-83. He captained his country in 48 Tests – an Australian record. By that time there were suggestions that, as a batsman, he was vulnerable against fast bowling early in his innings, yet he still scored two important centuries during the series, as he did against Pakistan in 1983-84.

He had made 7,110 runs in 87 Tests when he finally quit official international cricket in January 1984. However he said he would continue his career in cricket by playing for Queensland.

Trevor Chappell

Born: October 12, 1952, Unley,
  Adelaide, South Australia, Australia.
Height: 5ft 9in.   *Weight:* 11st 3lb.
Right-handed batsman, right-arm
  medium-paced bowler.
Teams: South Australia, Western
  Australia, New South Wales and
  Australia.

Career Highlights
1983: Hit 110 – Australia's only
  century of the tournament – in a
  World Cup group match against India
  at Nottingham.

Trevor is the third of the Chappell
brothers – and that is a difficult act to
follow! He did have his moment of
international glory when used as a
makeshift opener for the 1983 World
Cup, however.

He played his part in New South
Wales winning the Sheffield Shield in
1982-83 for the first time in 17
seasons, scoring 633 runs and finishing
third in the national bowling averages.
His three Tests were in England, 1981,
but he made just 79 runs.

Ewen Chatfield

Born: July 3, 1950, Dannevirke, New
  Zealand.

Trevor Chappell

Ewen Chatfield

Height: 6ft 4in.   *Weight:* 12st 7lb.
Right-arm fast medium bowler.
Teams: Wellington and New Zealand.

Career Highlights
1983: Took five for 95 against England
at Leeds.
1981-82: 51 wickets for Wellington
helped win Shell Trophy.

England's cricketers will always
remember Ewen Chatfield for an
horrific incident at Auckland in 1975,
when he had to be given the kiss of life
and heart massage by physio Bernie
Thomas, after being hit on the head by
a ball from Peter Lever. Chatfield was
making his debut then. Eight years
later the laboratory technician gave
England another reason to remember
him, when he bowled them out at
Leeds, to gain New Zealand their first
Test win in England and he played in
the return series in 1984.

Sylvester Clarke

Born: December 11, 1955, Lead Vale,
  Christchurch, Barbados.
Height: 6ft 1in.   *Weight:* 15st 0lb.
Right-arm fast bowler, right-handed
  batsman.
Teams: Barbados, Surrey, Transvaal
  and West Indies.

Career Highlights
1978: Performed hat trick for
  Barbados *v* Trinidad at Bridgetown.
1980: Another hat trick for Surrey *v*
  Nottinghamshire at the Oval.
1983: Best bowling: seven for 53
  against Warwickshire at the Oval.

Sylvester Clarke, a former carpenter
and a genuinely fast bowler, would
have played a prominent part in the
West Indies speed attack for some
years to come, had he not joined the
rebel tour to South Africa in 1983. At
that stage he had 42 wickets from 11
Tests. At that striking rate he would
get rich in South Africa, where he is
sponsored at £175 per wicket for
Transvaal!
   An effective 'slogger', his unbeaten
100 in 62 minutes for Surrey against
Glamorgan at Swansea was the fastest
century of the English season in 1981.

Jeremy Coney

Born: July 21, 1952, Wellington, New
  Zealand.
Height: 6ft 3in.   *Weight:* 13st 4lb.
Right-handed batsman, medium-
  paced bowler.
Teams: Wellington and New Zealand.

Career Highlights
1981-82: Captained Wellington to
  Shell Trophy victory.
1983: Topped country's batting in
  World Cup with 197 runs at 49.25,
  besides picking up nine wickets.

The bits and pieces player of the New
Zealand side since his debut as a 21-
year-old against Australia in 1974. He
has appeared in the last two World
Cups, in 1979 helping his country
reach the semi-finals.
   In the 1978-79 Test series against
Pakistan, he was New Zealand's most
successful batsman with 242 runs
(48.40).

Geoff Cook

Born: October 9, 1951,
  Middlesbrough, Cleveland, England.
Height: 6ft 0in.   *Weight:* 12st 10lb.
Right-handed batsman and slow left-
  arm bowler.
Teams: Northamptonshire, Eastern
  Province and England.

Career Highlights
1981: Amassed career best 1,759 runs
  in season for Northamptonshire.
1981-82: Toured India and Sri Lanka
  with England.
1982-83: Toured Australia and New
  Zealand with England.

Geoff Cook was given his England
chance after being proposed for a number of seasons (notably by the West
Indies captain, Clive Lloyd). However,
he managed only 203 runs in 13 innings and it seems that a potential captain has been lost to Test cricket. He
has been an impressive leader of
Northamptonshire since 1981, when
he took them to the NatWest Trophy
final, where he scored a fine 111
against Derbyshire. He is a brilliant
short leg fielder and occasional left-
arm spin bowler.
   Cook has played in South Africa for
Eastern Province, for whom he made
his highest first class score of 172
against Northern Transvaal at Port
Elizabeth, January 1980.

Geoff Cook

Nick Cook

Born: June 17, 1956, Leicester,
  Leicestershire, England.
Height: 6ft 0in.   *Weight:* 12st 0lb.
Left-arm spin bowler.
Teams: Leicestershire and England.

Career Highlights
1982: Claimed 90 wickets including
  seven for 63 against Somerset.
1983: Took five for 35 on Test debut
  against New Zealand at Lord's.

Nick Cook made a strikingly successful entry to Test cricket as an orthodox spin bowler when injury forced number one choice Phil Edmonds, to drop out. He took 17 wickets in two England matches and was selected for the winter tour to Pakistan and New Zealand. A calculating bowler, but an uncomplicated character, Cook had made steady progress in taking more than 350 wickets since his county debut in 1978.

Nick Cook

Norman Cowans

Norman Cowans

Born: April 17, 1961, Enfield St Mary,
   Jamaica.
Height: 6 ft 3 in.   *Weight:* 13 st 7 lb.
Right-arm fast bowler.
Teams: Middlesex and England.

Career Highlights
1982-83: Revived his own and
   England's fortunes on tour in
   Australia, taking six for 77 to set up a
   three-run victory at Melbourne.
1983: Took four for 39 to help
   Middlesex beat Essex in Benson and
   Hedges Cup final.

Cowans – Flash to his teammates – has
also earned his living as a squash and
real   tennis   professional   and   a
glassblower! He was picked out by
England's selectors as a fast bowler of
potential when they sent him on the
1982-83 tour and he retained his place
for the Pakistan and New Zealand trip
the following winter.
   The other high spot in his so-far
short career, was the Benson and
Hedges Cup final victory by Middlesex
over Essex in 1983. Hammered by a
rampant Graham Gooch in his first
spell, Cowans returned to pick up four
for 39 – for a three runs victory.

Colin Croft

Born: March 15, 1953, Demerara,
   British Guiana.
Height: 6 ft 4 in.   *Weight:* 14 st 0 in.
Right-arm fast bowler.
Teams: Guyana, Lancashire and West
   Indies.

Career Highlights
1977: Started Test career with 33
   wickets in home series against
   Pakistan, including eight for 29 in
   second Test at Port of Spain.

Colin Croft was one of the biggest

names to join the rebel West Indies team in South Africa in 1983. An airline pilot, who had also played for Kerry Packer in the seventies, Croft had taken 125 wickets in 27 Tests before his defection. He had two spells with Lancashire – 1977-78 and another season in 1982, when he was troubled by a back injury.

He earned infamy at Christchurch in 1980, when he appeared to barge into the umpire after being no-balled.

He earned sympathy at Capetown in 1983, when he was ordered out of a 'whites only' rail carriage during the second rebel tour.

Jeff Crowe

Born: September 14, 1958, Auckland, New Zealand.
Height: 5ft 11in.   *Weight:* 13st 7lb.
Right-handed batsman.
Teams: South Australia, Auckland and

Colin Croft

New Zealand.

Career Highlights
1981-82: Outstanding season in
Australia, when he scored 704 runs,
including three centuries, helping
South Australia win Sheffield Shield.

Jeff Crowe developed his obvious
natural talent in Australia, before
returning home to work for a finance
company and to claim a Test place in
1983 against Sri Lanka. He and
younger brother, Martin, first played
together at Test level against England
at the Oval, 1983.

Martin Crowe
Born: September 22, 1962, Auckland,
New Zealand.
Height: 6ft 2in.   *Weight:* 13st 10½lb.
Right-handed batsman, medium-
paced bowler.
Teams: Auckland, Somerset and New
Zealand.

Career Highlights
1982: Picked to play for New Zealand
at only 19, against Australia.

Martin Crowe has a copy-book technique and impressed, without scoring
heavily, on the 1983 tour to England.
First of the two Crowe brothers to be
picked for his country, although he is
four years younger than Jeff, he gained
experience of English conditions in
1982 by playing for Bradford in the
Yorkshire League.

Martin Crowe

Kevin Curran

Born: September 7, 1959, Rusape, Rhodesia.
Height: 6ft 1in.   *Weight:* 13st 3lb.
Right-handed batsman, right-arm fast medium bowler.
Team: Zimbabwe.

Career Highlights
1982: Helped Zimbabwe win ICC Trophy. Hit unbeaten 126 in group match against United States.

An aggressive batsman who went in down the order in the 1983 World Cup, making 73 off the eventual champions, India, at Tunbridge Wells. Kevin played as the professional for Rawtenstall in the Lancashire League. His father, also Kevin, appeared six times for Rhodesia between 1947 and 1954.

Kevin Curran

Wayne Daniel

Born: January 16, 1955, St Philip, Barbados.
Height: 6ft 1in.   *Weight:* 14st 2lb.
Right-arm fast bowler.
Teams: Barbados, Middlesex and West Indies.

Career Highlights
1976: Made Test debut against India and took four for 53 against England at Trent Bridge.
1978: For Middlesex, set a Benson and Hedges Cup bowling record of seven for 12 *v* Minor Counties East at Ipswich.

Wayne Daniel, a massively strong fast bowler, was signed by Middlesex in 1977, the previous year having impressed as a 20-year-old on the West Indies tour. Although he has contributed handsomely to Middlesex's run of success, he has been ignored by the West Indies, being recalled only in 1983 to their World Cup squad and for the tour of India. He, Michael Holding, Malcolm Marshall and Winston Davis linked up against the Indians to provide as fearsome a quartet of fast bowlers as even the West Indies have put out in recent seasons. Wayne passed 600 career wickets on the tour.

For Middlesex in 1980, he took 51 wickets in limited overs matches to equal the record of Robert Clapp (Somerset) set in 1974.

Rick Darling

Born: May 1, 1957, Waikerie, South Australia, Australia.
Height: 5ft 11½in.   *Weight:* 12st 0lb.
Right-handed batsman.
Teams: South Australia and Australia.

Career Highlights
1981-82: Topped the Australian

Wayne Daniel

national averages in 1981-82, with 1,011 runs at 72.23.

A great nephew of Joe Darling, who three times captained Australian teams in England at the turn of the century, Rick was elevated from batting No. 6 for his state to opening for Australia in 1977-78. He produced exciting flashes of form without building the long innings needed at Test level. His confidence was not increased when he was hit on the heart by England's Bob Willis at Adelaide in

Winston Davis

1979 and had to be revived by John Emburey, when gum Darling was chewing lodged in the back of his throat. The same year in Bombay he retired hurt in the sixth Test against India, when struck on the head by a delivery from Kapil Dev.

Winston Davis

Born: September 18, 1958, Kingstown, St. Vincent.
Height: 6ft 1in.   *Weight:* 11st 6lb.
Right-arm fast bowler.
Teams: Windward Islands, Glamorgan and West Indies.

Career Highlights
1982-83: Set Shell Shield record by taking 33 wickets in West Indian season.
1983: His seven for 41 against Australia at Leeds in World Cup is best bowling return in the competition.

Winston Davis is the latest in a seemingly endless supply of fast bowlers to come off the Caribbean assembly line. His performance in the 1982-83 season earned him his Test debut against India at Antigua and selection for the World Cup, at which he produced his record breaking performance against Australia. He went on West Indies 1983-84 tour to India.

He joined Glamorgan in 1982 and improved his personal best bowling performance in 1983, with seven for 50 against Nottinghamshire at Ebbw Vale.

Guy de Alwis

Born: February 15, 1960, Ceylon.
Height: 5ft 11½in.   *Weight:* 12st 8lb.
Wicket-keeper, right-handed batsman.
Team: Sri Lanka.

Career Highlights
1983: Topped Sri Lanka World Cup batting averages with 52.

He took over as Sri Lanka's first choice wicket-keeper after Mahes Goonatillake defected to South Africa. De Alwis made his Test debut in 1983 and that year showed his dual worth by topping the Sri Lanka batting averages in the World Cup.

Asantha de Mel

Born: May 9, 1959, Colombo, Ceylon.
Height: 5ft 10in.   *Weight:* 11st 6lb.
Right-arm fast medium bowler.
Teams: Sinhalese and Sri Lanka.

Career Highlights
1983: Joint leading wicket-taker in World Cup tournament, he and the Indian Roger Binny claiming 18 each.

Asantha de Mel is Sri Lanka's main strike bowler, who has improved since his country's entry to Test cricket in 1982 and many opponents were surprised by his pace in England in 1983.

Somachandra de Silva

Born: June 11, 1944, Galle, Ceylon.
Height: 5ft 8in.   *Weight:* 10st 9lb.
Right-arm leg spin bowler and right handed batsman.
Teams: Moratuwa and Sri Lanka.

Career Highlights
1979: Career best of eight for 46 for Sri Lankans against Oxford University at Guildford.
1982: Nine wickets in a Test match – against Pakistan at Faisalabad.

De Silva, known by his initials, D. S., is Sri Lanka's best all-round cricketer. A genuine leg-spin bowler and a compe-

Somachandra de Silva

tent enough batsman to hit 50's at Test level, he took over the Sri Lanka captaincy for two Tests against New Zealand in 1983.

He has played in all three World Cup tournaments and is a well known figure in English Minor Counties cricket, having represented Lincolnshire and Shropshire. In the Central Lancashire League, he took 114 wickets and made 951 runs for Middleston in 1982.

Roy Dias

Born: September 18, 1952, Colombo, Ceylon.
Height: 5ft 6in.   *Weight:* 10st 0lb.
Right-handed batsman.
Teams: Sinhalese and Sri Lanka.

Career Highlights
1982: Scored his maiden Test century (109) in Sri Lanka's fourth match against Pakistan at Lahore.

Roy Dias was an automatic choice when Sri Lanka gained entry to Test cricket in 1982 and, although he failed with a duck in his first innings against England, he was soon looking comfortable against international opposition. He made a century and four 50's in his first half-a-dozen Tests. A keen cover fielder, he was vice-captain of the 1983 World Cup team.

Graham Dilley

Born: May 18, 1959, Dartford, Kent, England.
Height: 6ft 4in.   *Weight:* 14st 5lb.
Right-arm fast bowler and left-handed batsman.

Roy Dias

Teams: Kent and England.

Career Highlights
1979-80: Youngest cricketer to be picked for England for 30 years when he made his debut on tour to Australia, five months before his 21st birthday.
1980: Voted Young Cricketer of the Year.
1981: Topped England's bowling averages against Australia, and in that series shared a match-turning stand of 117 for eighth wicket with Ian Botham at Leeds.

Graham Dilley has the speed and the physique – but has he the mental attitude and technique needed for a lasting England career? This is the question experts have asked since the big, blond fast bowler burst on the international scene. His progress, both for England and Kent, has been hampered by injury and by a chest-on action which irritates the purists. He was dropped for the 1982-83 winter tour, but was back in the England camp for the World Cup and went on the 1984 trip to Pakistan and New Zealand.

If he can establish himself as a new ball bowler, England's batting will also be extended because Dilley has already shown himself a clean, left-handed striker of the ball and capable of scoring 50s at Test level. He works as a diamond cutter.

Graham Dilley

Dilip Doshi

Dilip Doshi

Born: December 22, 1947, Rajkot,
  India.
Height: 5 ft 10 in.   *Weight:* 11 st 0 lb.
Slow left-arm bowler.
Teams: Bengal, Nottinghamshire,
  Warwickshire and India.

Career Highlights
1980: Took six for 103 on Test debut
  against Australia at Madras and in
  England claimed 101 victims for
  Warwickshire.

A varied career was climaxed for Dilip
Doshi when he finally won Test
recognition at the age of 32. He had
long been kept out of the Indian side
by the great Bishan Bedi, but Dilip
seized his opportunity to take 27 wickets in his first series.

However, the signs are that he will
be caught between two generations.
He reached 100 wickets in his 28th
Test and then was dropped in favour of
the teenaged Maninder Singh.

Dilip has done the rounds in
English cricket. Apart from two spells
at Notts and one at Warwickshire, he
has played for Sussex and Lancashire
2nd XIs, Meltham in the Huddersfield
League, and Hertfordshire and
Northumberland in the Minor
Counties.

Paul Downton

Born: April 4, 1957, Farnborough,
  Kent, England.
Height: 5ft 10in.   *Weight:* 11st 9lb.
Wicket-keeper and right-handed
  batsman.
Teams: Kent, Middlesex and England.

Career Highlights
1981: Four Tests for England.

At only 20, and with just seven first
class games for Kent behind him, law
student Paul Downton was pinpointed
as England's wicket-keeper of the
future. He was picked to understudy
Bob Taylor on the 1977-78 tour of
Pakistan and New Zealand. He got his
England chance in 1981, by which time
he had moved to Middlesex, and was
dropped after four Tests. However, he
was back in the England reckoning in
1984, when he was on stand-by for the
winter tour.

His father, George, kept wicket for
Kent.

Paul Downton

Jeff Dujon

Born: May 28, 1956, Jamaica.
Height: 5ft 10½in.   *Weight:* 10st 6lb.
Wicket-keeper and right-handed
  batsman.
Teams: Jamaica and West Indies.

Career Highlights
1981-82: Emerged at Test level on
  West Indies tour of Australia.
1983: Scored maiden Test century
  (110) at Antigua.

Dujon played his first two Tests as a
specialist batsman, being good enough
in 1981 to score an unbeaten 135 for
Jamaica *v* Barbados in the Shell
Shield. The way was cleared for him to
continue behind the stumps in 1983,
when David Murray was banned for
joining the rebel West Indian tour to
South Africa. Dujon claimed 19 victims in the 1983 home series against
India, as well as averaging over 50 with
the bat. He was first choice for that
year's World Cup tournament and
retained his place for the tour of India.

John Dyson

Born: June 11, 1954, Sydney, New
  South Wales, Australia.
Height: 5ft 11in.   *Weight:* 12st 0lb.
Right-handed batsman.
Teams: New South Wales and
  Australia.

Career Highlights
1979: 197 for New South Wales
  against Tasmania at Sydney.
1980-81: Scored 1,028 runs in
  Australian season.
1982: Opened in all five Tests for
  Australia's Ashes-winning team.

An unspectacular batsman, who has
both opened and gone in No. 3 for his
country, John Dyson had his first

Jeff Dujon

chance at Test level during the days of
Kerry Packer. That was in 1977. He
finally made his maiden Test century
against England with 102 at Leeds in
1981 and followed this up with an
unbeaten 127 against West Indies at
Sydney the following winter.

However, after 27 Test matches he
was still averaging less than 30 and the
selectors appeared to lose faith in him
in 1983.

Bruce Edgar

Bruce Edgar

Born: November 23, 1956, Wellington,
New Zealand.
Height: 6ft 0in.   *Weight:* 12st 10lb.
Left-handed batsman.
Teams: Wellington and New Zealand.

Career Highlights
1982: Scored 161 against Australia at
Auckland.
1983: New Zealand's leading run-
getter in series in England, with 336
in four Tests.

Bruce Edgar showed early maturity on
his first tour of England in 1978 and
since then, this chartered accountant
has continued to ally a cool temperament to skill as an opening batsman.
He passed 1,000 runs in his 17th Tests
match. Against Australia in Wellington,
1982, he displayed great concentration
when taking 336 minutes over 55.

Phil Edmonds

Born: March 18, 1951, Lusaka,
Zambia.
Height: 6ft 2in.   *Weight:* 14st 0lb.
Left-arm spin bowler and right-handed
batsman.
Teams: Middlesex, Cambridge Univer-
sity, Eastern Province and England.

Career Highlights
1975: Took five for 28 on his Test
debut at Leeds against Australia,
including wickets of Ian and Greg
Chappell.
1978: Took seven for 66 against
Pakistan at Karachi in January.
1981: Did the hat trick against
Leicestershire at Leicester.

Phil Edmonds is one of the enigmas of
cricket, or so the actions of the
England selectors over the years would
suggest. Up to the end of the 1983

season he had played only 23 Tests,
despite his obvious all-round talent as
a genuine spin bowler, a batsman good
enough to have a first class score of
141 not out to his credit, and an
athletic fielder.

A former Cambridge University
captain, he has a lively, independent
mind as well as a reputation as a mis-
chievous influence in the dressing
room. His insistence on all points of
view being aired earned him the nickname 'Maggie' (at that time Mrs
Thatcher led the opposition)!

He was bitterly disappointed at
being omitted from England's winter
tour to Pakistan and New Zealand
after losing his Test place during the
summer because of injury. Voted
Young Cricketer of the Year 1974, he
served under Mike Brearley as Middlesex vice-captain in 1970.

Phil Edmonds

John Emburey batting.

Jock Edwards

Born: May 27, 1955, Nelson, New
    Zealand.
Height: 5ft 7½in.   *Weight:* 12st 10lb.
Right-handed batsman, wicket-keeper.
Teams: Central Districts and New
    Zealand.

Career Highlights
1978: Toured England.

A happy-go-lucky cricketer who was
first picked for his country as a batsman, but was later entrusted with
wicket-keeping duties. On the 1978
tour to England, Jock was dropped
after a fumbling performance behind
the stumps in the second Test at Nottingham. A broken leg ruled him out of
contention for the 1983 World Cup,
but he resumed playing at the start of
the 1983-84 season.

John Emburey

Born: August 20, 1952, Peckham,
    London, England.
Height: 6ft 2in.   *Weight:* 13st 7lb.
Right-arm off-spin bowler and right-
    handed batsman.
Teams: Middlesex, Western Province
    and England.

Career Highlights
1978: Made Test debut against New
    Zealand.
1979: Played an important part in
    England's sucess in Australia, with
    16 wickets in series.
1982: Took Test best of six for 33
    against Sri Lanka.
1983: First bowler to take 100 wickets
    in that English season.

The ban on the rebels who toured
South Africa has robbed the England
team of its first-choice spinner in John
Emburey. He had firmly established

Duncan Fletcher

himself in that position by 1982 and a further irony was that he produced his best return at international level (against Sri Lanka) in his final match for England before the ban.

The enduring Fred Titmus prevented Emburey from gaining a regular first team spot with Middlesex until his mid-twenties. But since 1977, Emburey and his spin partner Phil Edmonds have ensured Middlesex of continuing success, with three County Championships, two Gillette Cups and a Benson and Hedges triumph. They have been equally adept whether required to defend in the one-day competitions or attack on the last day of a Championship match.

By 1983, Emburey was in the genuine all-rounder category. He passed 100 wickets for the first time (final total 103), scored 782 runs (top score 133 against eventual champions Essex) and took 23 catches (mostly in the gulley).

He has been more vociferous, publicly, than his 14 colleagues who took South Africa's money. *'The three year ban was much longer than we expected,'* he has said. *'What sickens me is that South Africans are in the England side ... Lamb and Smith were after all brought up in the South African system.'*

Duncan Fletcher

Born: September 27, 1948, Salisbury, Rhodesia.
Height: 5ft 11in.   *Weight:* 12st 2lb.
Left-handed batsman, right-arm fast-medium bowler.
Teams: Rhodesia and Zimbabwe.

Career Highlights
1982: Under his command, Zimbabwe won ICC Trophy.
1983: Led Zimbabwe to biggest upset

in three World Cup tournaments, when they beat Australia by 13 runs at Nottingham.

Duncan Fletcher showed himself to be an all-round cricketer of great ability during the 1983 World Cup, although his exploits came as no surprise to those who have followed the game in Africa. He has played over 100 first class matches for Rhodesia and now Zimbabwe, and his record in 1983 stood at more than 3,700 runs and over 200 wickets. After the World Cup, he retired from the Zimbabwe captaincy, having led his country for four seasons.

He first played Currie Cup cricket for Rhodesia in the 1969-70 season and in 1975 produced his best bowling of six for 31 (11 for 92 in the match) against Eastern Province at Bulawayo. In 1977 he appeared as the professional for Rishton in the Lancashire League, completing the double of 1,000 runs and 50 wickets, and that season he also scored three centuries for Cambridgeshire in the Minor Counties Championship.

He topped Zimbabwe's batting in the 1983 World Cup, his innings including 71 not out against West Indies and an unbeaten 69 and four wickets in the famous victory against Australia. He plays his club cricket for Old Hararians.

Keith Fletcher

Born: May 20, 1944, Worcester,
  Worcestershire, England.
Height: 5ft 10½in.   *Weight:* 10st 7lb.
Right-handed batsman and occasional
  leg-break bowler.
Teams: Essex and England.

Career Highlights
1973: Set record fifth wicket stand for
  England in all Tests when he and

Tony Greig put on 254 against India at Bombay.

1975: Registered highest Test score of 216 at Auckland in February, when he and Mike Denness added 266 for the fourth wicket, a record for England *v* New Zealand.

1976: Scored two centuries in a match – 111 and 102 not out – *v* Notts at Nottingham.

1981-82: Captain of England in India and Sri Lanka.

Keith Fletcher paid dearly for one flash of temper while he was captain of England. During a niggling and tedious series with India, he was given out caught behind the wicket in the second Test at Bangalore during December 1981. Fletcher showed what he thought of the decision by knocking the stumps over with his bat. By summer England had a new chairman of selectors, Peter May, who was already making loud noises about 'discipline' and 'standards'. Fletcher was replaced as captain of his country by fast bowler Bob Willis, and his Test career was surely ended after 59 Tests – seven as captain – and seven full tours.

It had begun in 1968, with a duck against Australia at Leeds. He went on to score 3,272 runs (average 39.90) with seven centuries. Many of his better innings were played to save, rather than win, matches. In 1974 against Pakistan at the Oval, he scored the slowest Test century in England, taking 458 minutes to reach three figures. However, his caution was justified; England drew after Pakistan had topped 600. The Gnome, as he is known throughout the game, made his Essex debut in 1962. Now, with the retirement of Mike Brearley, Fletcher is widely regarded as the best tactician among English county captains. He continued to lead Essex through the most successful period of their history with professionalism and flair and his determination was proven once again in 1983, when he took them to a second County Championship with a late surge. He has also led them to the Benson and Hedges Cup and Sunday League title. In 1983 Fletcher passed a career total of 32,000 runs.

His favourite relaxations are fishing, shooting and gardening.

Neil Foster

Born: May 6, 1962, Colchester, Essex, England.
Height: 6ft 3in.   *Weight:* 12st 7lb.
Right-arm fast bowler.
Teams: Essex and England.

Career Highlights

1983: His 52 wickets put Essex on the way to their second County Championship. Made debut for England against New Zealand at Lord's.

1984: Took six for 30 for England *v* Northern Districts, in Hamilton, New Zealand.

Such was the rise of Neil Foster, that in three years this promising fast bowler graduated from the classroom to the England dressing room. He made his Essex debut in 1980, answering an emergency call to the Philip Morant Comprehensive School in Colchester, where he was studying for his 'A' levels. He promptly took three for 51 in his first match against Kent.

He was given a regular chance with Essex in 1983, seizing his opportunity so well that England picked him, too. He suffered a stress fracture to his back in 1982, rectified by the insertion of a steel plate which had to be removed before Foster set off on England's winter tour of 1984.

Foster/Fowler/Franklin

Graeme Fowler

Graeme Fowler

Born: April 20, 1957, Accrington,
  Lancashire, England.
Height: 5ft 9in.   *Weight:* 10st 7lb.
Left-handed batsman and emergency
  wicket-keeper.
Teams: Lancashire and England.

Career Highlights
1981: Scored 1,560 runs in season for
  Lancashire.
1982: Scored two centuries in a match
  – 126 and 128 not out – against
  Warwickshire at Southport. In Test
  debut against Pakistan at Leeds
  scored 86 runs.
1983: Hit first 100 for England when
  he and Chris Tavare set a record
  opening stand against New Zealand
  with 223 at the Oval. Averaged 51.96
  for the season, scoring 1,403 runs.

A nimble, left-handed opening batsman, whose ability to keep wicket earned him the role of deputy to Bob Taylor on England's 1984 tour to Pakistan and New Zealand. Since his England debut, he has managed enough runs (often in the second innings) to earn an extended trial, although some experts criticise his technique.

However, he has great confidence in his ability and could form an attractive opening partnership with Graham Gooch, when that player completes a three-year ban for his part in the South African escapade.

At 15, Fowler was the youngest opener in the Lancashire League. He went on to play for England Schools and Young England.

Trevor Franklin

Born: March 15, 1962, Auckland, New
  Zealand.
Height: 6ft 4¾in.   *Weight:* 13st 2lb.

57

Teams: Auckland and New Zealand.

Career Highlights
1983: Test debut.

Played in Auckland's victorious Shell Trophy team as an 18-year-old opening batsman and made his Test debut at Nottingham in 1983. Franklin, a sales representative for a towel firm, scored 76 in guiding Auckland to their Shell victory against Northern Districts.

Roy Fredericks

Born: November 11, 1942, Blairmount, Berbice, British Guiana.
Height: 5ft 4in.   *Weight:* 10st 2lb.
Left-handed batsman, slow left-arm bowler.
Teams: Guyana, Glamorgan and West Indies.

Career Highlights
1975: Played one of the great Test innings at Perth when, opening for West Indies against Australia, he reached a century off 71 balls in 116 minutes, going on to make 169 with a six and 27 fours.

Roy Fredericks was an opening batsman in 59 Tests for West Indies between 1968 and 1977, when he joined World Series Cricket. He then became Minister for Sport in his native Guyana, but returned to first class cricket with startling success in 1983. He helped Guyana win the Shell Shield for the first time in eight years with scores of 103 against Trinidad & Tobago and 217 off Jamaica.

He played three seasons with Glamorgan between 1971 and 1973, in the second contributing an unbeaten 228 to the county's record opening stand of 330, which he set with Alan Jones against Northants at Swansea.

Anshuman Gaekwad

Born: September 23, 1952, Bombay, India.
Height: 6ft 0in.   *Weight:* 11st 0lb.
Right-handed batsman, off-spin bowler.
Teams: Barado and India

Career Highlights
1983: Scored 201 against Pakistan at Jalandhar.

Anshuman Gaekwad is the son of Datta, himself a former Test player who captained India in England in 1959.

Anshuman's Test days seemed to be over after a disappointing trip to England in 1979, but he earned a recall with some outstanding performances for Baroda in the 1982-83 Ranji Trophy, including 225 *v* Gujarat. He occasionally bowls his off breaks in Test matches.

He has the dubious distinction of having scored the slowest double century in first-class cricket – 652 minutes and 426 balls – against Pakistan, at Jalandhar, in 1983.

Joel Garner

Born: December 16, 1952, Barbados.
Height: 6ft 8in.   *Weight:* 17st 0lb.
Right-arm fast bowler, right-handed batsman.
Teams: Barbados, Somerset, South Australia and West Indies.

Career Highlights
1979: Helped his country win World Cup final against England with five for 38.
1980: Took six for 56 for West Indies against New Zealand, at Auckland.

Joel 'Big Bird' Garner is one of the most successful cricketers playing, a

Joel Garner

matchwinner for West Indies, Barbados (whom he has helped to six Shell Shield titles since 1976) and Somerset (who have taken the Sunday League, the Gillette Cup, the Benson and Hedges Cup twice and the NatWest Trophy since he joined them full-time.

His extraordinary build (he takes custom made size 16 boots) presents two main problems for batsman – sighting the ball when it is delivered from the hand of a 6ft 8in giant, and trying to deal with the steep bounce. He is very rarely hit out of the attack, which makes him especially useful in limited overs cricket.

His accuracy was well demonstrated in the 1979 World Cup final at Lord's, when four of his five victims were bowled. He was even more devastating in that year's Gillette final, with six for 29 to land Somerset victory over Northants. He gave his adopted county Benson and Hedges victory in successive years at Lord's, with five for only 14 against Surrey in 1981 and three wickets against Somerset in 1982.

He was bothered by a knee injury in 1983 and decided to take a rest from Test cricket in the 1983-84 winter, missing West Indies tour of India.

Mike Gatting

Mike Gatting

Born: June 6, 1957, Kingsbury,
    London, England.
Height: 5ft 10in.   *Weight:* 13st 8lb.
Right-handed batsman and medium-
    pace bowler.
Teams: Middlesex and England.

Career Highlights
1981: Voted Young Cricketer of the
    Year. Played in all six Tests when
    England won Ashes.
1983: Produced his most authoritative
    Test innings to date with 81 (13
    fours) against New Zealand at
    Lord's. Top Englishman in first class
    averages with 1,494 runs at an
    average of 64.95. Was appointed
    Middlesex captain in succession to
    Mike Brearley and led them to
    Benson and Hedges Cup final victory
    at Lord's.

Mike Gatting, one of English county
cricket's most prolific batsmen, has
struggled to produce the same fluency
at international level. He did not
manage one century in his first 20
Tests. Gatting is at a loss to explain the
disparity, pointing out that he has
scored good runs against most of the
world's leading bowlers in the English
county game.

He has been in and out of the
England team since his debut as a 20-
year-old against Pakistan at Karachi in
1978. Yet in consecutive seasons from
1981 he always averaged over 50 with
his pugnacious batting. His highest
score is 192 *v* Surrey at the Oval, 1982.
He is a genuine, medium-paced bowler
and always an alert fielder. England's
selectors would dearly like him to
establish himself as a batsman; his promising first season in charge of Middlesex suggests that Gatting could
provide them with one option when
Bob Willis is replaced as captain.

Gatting's brother, Steve, is a professional footballer, and appeared in the 1983 FA Cup final for Brighton.

Sunil Gavaskar

Born: July 10, 1949, Bombay, India.
Height: 5ft 5in.   *Weight:* 10st 5lb.
Right-handed batsman.
Teams: Bombay, Somerset and India.

Career Highlights
1979: Gavaskar and Dilip Vengsarkar added an Indian second wicket record of 344 (unbroken) against West Indies at Calcutta.
1981-82: Hit career best score of 340 batting for Bombay against Bengal.
1983: Became highest scoring Test batsman of all time at Ahmedabad during his innings of 90 against West Indies, when he passed previous best of 8,114 set by Geoff Boycott. He went on to pass Sir Donald Bradman's record of 29 Test centuries.

The little master of the modern game had the modesty to admit, when he drew alongside Bradman's total of 29 Test centuries: *'I am obviously very pleased, but I do not regard this as equalling his record. Bradman scored his runs in 52 Test matches, and I am playing my 95th.'*

What Gavaskar didn't mention was that his runs have been scored as an opener (while Bradman was usually protected from the new ball) and in a side that has often been struggling. During his long international career, he has fully lived up to the billing he earned himself in his first Test series, in West Indies in 1971. Then he hit 774 runs and four 100s, although he played only four times, helping India to their first win in a rubber against West Indies. At Port of Spain he scored 124 and 220 not out.

He has captained India in 40 Tests. His uncle, Madhav Mantri, was a wicket-keeper/batsman who played four times for India in the fifties.

One of his greatest innings was played in 1979, when he scored 221 for India at the Oval as his country failed by only nine runs to reach a fourth innings target of 438 to beat England.

Sunil Gavaskar

Norman Gifford MBE

Born: March 30, 1940, Ulverston,
  Lancashire, England.
Height: 5ft 10in.   *Weight:* 13st 7lb.
Slow left-arm bowler and left-handed
  batsman.
Teams: Worcestershire, Warwickshire
  and England.

Career Highlights
1961: Took 133 wickets at an average
  of 19.66 for Worcestershire.
1964-73: Played 15 Tests for England,
  with a best return of five for 55
  against Pakistan at Karachi in 1973.
1974: Captained Worcestershire to the
  Championship.

The 1983 English season was a
remarkable one for 43-year-old Norman Gifford, who was released by Worcestershire and started a new career
with Warwickshire. The oldest player
in the championship, he proceeded to
bowl more overs than anyone else
(1,043) and for the fourth time in his
life topped 100 wickets. His performance helped Warwickshire, bottom of
the County Championship in 1982, to
rise to fifth.

Gifford, whose England career was
limited by Derek Underwood's
excellence, took 33 wickets in his 15
Tests. On the 1982 and 1983 England
tours, he has served as England's
assistant manager.

Larry Gomes

Born: July 13, 1953, Arima, Trinidad.
Height: 5ft 10in.   *Weight:* 10st 8lb.
Left-handed batsman, right-arm
  medium-paced or off-spin bowler.
Teams: Middlesex, Trinidad and West
  Indies.

Career Highlights
1981-82: Topped West Indies' batting

Larry Gomes

on tour to Australia with 712 runs,
393 of them in the three Tests. Hit
unbeaten 200 against Queensland.

Larry Gomes, a slightly built left-
hander, has established himself in the
West Indies team with the departure of
Alvin Kallicharran. He played at Middlesex between 1973 and 1976, but
never gained a regular place; in fact he
failed to score a single century. He was
on the 1976 West Indies tour to
England, but failed in two Tests.

He got a second chance when the
Packer players withdrew halfway
through the 1978 home series against
Australia and promptly made 101 at
Georgetown and 115 at Kingston,
Jamaica. He again demonstrated his
partiality to Australian bowling with
two more centuries in the short series
in 1981-82.

Gomes passed 10,000 runs in his career during the 1983 tour of India. That year he also had a successful World Cup with 258 runs, average 64.50. West Indies have made considerable use of his bowling, especially in limited overs cricket.

Playing as a professional for Oldham in the Central Lancashire League, he had a phenomenal season in 1982 with 1,459 runs plus 103 wickets.

Graham Gooch

Born: July 23, 1953, Leytonstone, London, England.
Height: 6ft 0in. *Weight:* 13st 0lb.
Right-handed batsman and medium-paced bowler.
Teams: Essex, Western Province and England.

Career Highlights
1978: Set Essex second wicket record of 321 with Ken McEwan v Northants at Ilford.
1979: Starred in Essex's Benson and Hedges Cup final victory over Surrey at Lord's, unleashing a magnificent 120, with three sixes and 11 fours – it was the first century scored in all eight Benson and Hedges finals.
1981: Hit best Test score of 153 v West Indies in Kingston, Jamaica, reaching his century out of 155 in 40 overs.
1982: Took seven for 14 v Worcestershire at Ilford; recorded highest score in one-day match in England with 198 not out in the Benson and Hedges match against Sussex at Hove.
1983: Scored 163 and put on 283 for the first wicket with Lawrence Seeff

Graham Gooch

for Western Province against Eastern Province at Capetown. This set a Western Province record for any partnership.

Graham Gooch is probably the greatest loss to the England team of the 15 players banned for three years for the unofficial tour to South Africa in 1982. He had become one of the game's most commanding batsmen, an opener capable of dominating even the most dangerous fast bowlers with his powerful driving and forceful shots square of the wicket.

When he made his England debut in 1975 against Australia he was 21 and his rawness showed against a bowling side spearheaded by Lillee and Thomson. He failed with a 'pair' and after one more match was rested from the Test scene for three years, by which time he had been promoted from the middle order to open for Essex. He still needed time to adjust to international cricket and did not score his maiden Test century until his 36th innings, against the West Indies at Lord's in 1980. He struck 123 out of 165, with a 6 and 17 4s. The following winter he was again impressive against the same opponents. He hit 460 runs and two centuries in the series, while a year later, on England's difficult tour of India he showed that he could also handle high class spin. Gooch is a medium-paced change bowler who has also proved penetrative in 'swing' conditions.

Graham's love of cricket was fostered by his father, Alf, who played for East Ham Corinthians. Graham had ambitions as a wicket-keeper/batsman, but dropped this dual role when he entered the Essex 2nd team in 1973. He helped them win the 2nd XI championship, scoring 265 runs and taking 34 wickets.

Ian Gould

Born: August 19, 1957, Slough, Buckinghamshire, England.
Height: 5ft 7in.   *Weight:* 11st 7lb.
Wicket-keeper and left-handed batsman.
Teams: Middlesex, Sussex and Auckland.

Career Highlights
1982-83: Went on England's tour of Australia and New Zealand.
1983: Kept wicket in World Cup.

Ian Gould was forced to move from Middlesex when they signed Paul Downton as their first choice 'keeper from Kent. Ian switched to Sussex in 1981. He is a good enough batsman to have scored 128 *v* Worcestershire in 1978 and to have opened in one day internationals on tour for England.

David Gower

Born: April 1, 1957, Tunbridge Wells, Kent, England.
Height: 5ft 11¾in.   *Weight:* 11st 11lb.
Left-handed batsman.
Teams: Leicestershire and England.

Career Highlights
1979: Hit 200 not out for England against India at Birmingham.
1981: With Chris Balderstone put on an unbroken 289 for Leicestershire against Essex, a county record for second wicket.
1983: Most prolific batsman from any country in World Cup with 384 runs, (average 76.80).

David Gower is an accomplished stroke-maker, who has enjoyed a reputation as England's golden boy since his international debut in 1978, making 58 in his first innings (against Pakistan) and getting 111 later that

Ian Gould

David Gower

summer against New Zealand at the Oval. He was 21 years and 119 days and thus replaced Peter May (who was 91 days older) as England's youngest post-war centurion.

He was appointed England's vice-captain in 1982 and looks a good bet to take over from Bob Willis, especially as he will gain experience in 1984, when he becomes Leicestershire's leader.

The blond bachelor boy has had to live with one or two disappointments since his initial success. His progress at one stage did not match his poten-

tial. And England dropped him during the home series of 1980 against West Indies and, again, the following year for the final Test against Australia. However, he enjoyed three consistently good tours – West Indies, 1981; India and Sri Lanka, 1981-82; and Australia and New Zealand, 1982-83. By the 1983 home series he was recognised as one of the world's finest batsmen, hitting successive centuries against New Zealand following on from his run-gathering World Cup.

A brilliant fielder, he and Derek Randall have saved many runs for

England on both sides of the wicket.

Gower spent his early years in East Africa, where his father was in the Colonial Service. The Leicestershire connection began when his father became registrar of Loughborough College. David was educated at King's School, Canterbury, and won a place at London University to read law. However, he had enough faith in his sporting ability to opt for cricket.

He has explained: *'People were advising me to go to university to get some kind of career behind me. But I was bored by a lot of the law course.'*

He has certainly never bored spectators at cricket matches. By the end of the 1983 season, his 53 Test appearances had yielded 3,742 runs (average 43.01).

A squash player, he relaxes from sport by listening to classical music.

Evan Gray

Born: November 18, 1954, Wellington, New Zealand.
Height: 6ft 1in.　*Weight:* 13st 2lb.
Right-handed batsman, slow-left arm bowler.
Teams: Wellington and New Zealand.

Career Highlights
1983: Made Test debut at Lord's against England and took three for 73 in second innings.

Evan Gray has built a reputation as a more-than-useful all-rounder in New Zealand. In Wellington's Shell Trophy triumphs in 1981-82, he scored 623 runs and took 24 wickets. He was given a chance at international level at the age of 28 and played two Tests on the 1983 tour to England. He had gained experience of English conditions in the Lancashire League, taking 69 wickets in the 1982 season.

Alvin Greenidge

Born: August 20, 1956, St Lawrence, Barbados.
Height: 6ft 1in.　*Weight:* 12st 8lb.
Right-handed batsman.
Teams: Barbados and West Indies.

Career Highlights
1982: Scored 172 for Barbados *v* Jamaica, at Bridgetown.

Alvin Greenidge, no relation to Gordon, played six Tests during the Packer period of 1978-79. He scored 56 in his first innings, against Australia at Georgetown, and followed this up with 69 in his second Test. Although he continued to be a consistent scorer with the powerful Barbados side, he faded from the Test scene once the Packerites returned. In 1983, Greenidge joined the rebel West Indian tour of South Africa.

Gordon Greenidge

Born: May 1, 1951, St Peter, Barbados.
Height: 5ft 10in.　*Weight:* 13st 7lb.
Right-handed batsman.
Teams: Hampshire, Barbados and West Indies.

Career Highlights
1974: First West Indian to score a century on Test debut overseas with 107 against India, at Bangalore.
1976: Scored two centuries in a Test match, 134 and 101 *v* England at Manchester. Hit 1,952 runs that season with Hampshire.

Gordon Greenidge is the fastest scoring opening batsman currently playing Test cricket. He might have represented England, qualifying by residence after emigrating from the West Indies with his parents when he was 12 and going to school in Reading. But he opted for his native West Indies and struck up a fine partnership with the left-handed Roy Fredericks and, more recently, Desmond Haynes.

Greenidge is a fearsome driver of the ball and he is prepared to go for his considerable range of shots from the first ball of an innings, a habit he may well have picked up from another of his partners, the South African Barry Richards, with whom he played at Hampshire during the 1970s.

He averages over 40 and improved his best score for West Indies to 194 against India at Kanpur, 1983. His style is particularly suited to the one-day game and he holds individual batting records for the Sunday League (163 not out against Warwickshire in 1979) and for the Gillette Cup, now the NatWest Trophy (177 *v* Glamorgan in 1975).

Gordon Greenidge

Ian Greig

Born: December 8, 1955, Queenstown, South Africa.
Height: 5ft 11½in.   *Weight:* 12st 7lb.
Right-handed batsman and medium-paced bowler.
Teams: Border, Griqualand West, Sussex, Cambridge University and England.

Career Highlights
1979: Captained Cambridge University, where he won three blues for cricket and two for Rugby.
1981: Took 79 wickets and scored 911 runs for Sussex. Against Hampshire, scored 119 not out and took six for 75 and four for 57.
1982: Took four for 53 against Pakistan on Test debut at Birmingham.

Ian is the brother of former England captain Tony and followed him into the England team with two appearances against Pakistan in 1982. A useful all-rounder, but without the same competitive streak which marked Tony's game. Although he was exposed at Test level first time round, he may fight his way back, as did Greig senior. Ian has played in South Africa for Border and Griqualand West.

Richard Hadlee

Born: July 3, 1951, Christchurch, New Zealand.
Height: 6ft 1in.   *Weight:* 11st 9lb.
Right-arm fast bowler, left-handed batsman.
Teams: Nottinghamshire, Canterbury, Tasmania and New Zealand.

Career Highlights
1971-72: Took hat trick for Canterbury against Central Districts in his debut season.

Ian Greig

Richard Hadlee in action

1974: Took seven wickets when New Zealand beat Australia for first time at Christchurch in March 1974.
1976: His own, and New Zealand's, best bowling was seven for 23 against India at Wellington. Shared New Zealand's record seventh wicket stand of 186 with Warren Lees against Pakistan at Karachi.
1978: Bowled England out for 64 in the second innings with six for 26.
1980: Scored his maiden Test century (103) *v* West Indies at Christchurch.
1983: Leading bowler in World Cup with 14 wickets at 12.85. Topped New Zealand's batting in the four-match series against England (301 runs at 50.17).

Richard Hadlee has been New Zealand's most effective bowler and vies with their former captain, John Reid, for the accolade as his country's greatest-ever all-rounder. Hadlee's batting has improved tremendously in recent years and after 44 Tests he boasted the fine record of 210 wickets and 1,601 runs. Against England in 1983, he became only the ninth player to complete the Test double of 150 wickets and 1,500 runs (following Vinoo Mankad, Keith Miller, Richie Benaud, Ray Lindwall, Gary Sobers, Ian Botham, Kapil Dev and Imran Khan).

Richard is the fourth son of Walter Hadlee, who captained the 1949 New Zealanders in England and who has since played a leading role in cricket administration. Two other sons have risen to prominence at international level, Dayle playing in 26 Tests and Barry being a member of the 1975 World Cup squad. Richard's wife Karen, who bats and is a medium-paced bowler, has played for the New Zealand women's team.

Hadlee's skill and aggression have

Hadlee dispatches another batsman

been among the main factors in New Zealand's increasing competitiveness during the Seventies and Eighties. He possesses a classic fast bowling action and is able to maintain considerable speed off an economical, shortened run.

John Hampshire

Born: February 10, 1941, Thurnscoe, Yorkshire, England.
Height: 6ft 0in.   *Weight:* 13st 0lb.
Right-handed batsman.
Teams: Yorkshire, Derbyshire, Tasmania and England.

Career Highlights
1969: Scored 107 on Test debut at Lord's against West Indies; he and Australian Harry Graham (1893) are only players to have achieved this feat at cricket's headquarters.
1978: Best county season with 1,596 runs for Yorkshire at an average of 53.20.
1979-80: Captained Yorkshire.

John Hampshire's future at international level looked assured when, in 1969, he displayed the skill and the nerve to score 107 in his first Test innings including 15 fours. However, he

John Hampshire

never showed that form for England again, totalling 403 runs in eight appearances, although, at the start of their careers many good judges had thought him at least the equal of his Yorkshire contemporary Geoff Boycott.

By the time he left Yorkshire in 1981, having captained them for a couple of seasons, he had passed a total of 25,000 runs. He played out the autumn of his career with neighbours Derbyshire.

Haroon Rashid

Born: March 25, 1953, Pakistan.
Height: 5ft 11in.   *Weight:* 12st 7lb.
Right-handed batsman.
Teams: Karachi, Sind, National Bank, PIA, United Bank and Pakistan.

Career Highlights
1977-78: Scored centuries in successive matches in home series against England.

Haroon took advantage of his chance in the Pakistan team during the Packer era, but has been unable to maintain his promise. He had a dismal time on Pakistan's return tour to England in 1978 and has struggled to gain a regular place in a strong batting side. He reminded everyone of his ability on hard wickets with 153 against Sri Lanka at Karachi, in 1982, but failed again in English conditions in the summer of that year. He is an exceptional short-leg fielder.

Frank Hayes

Born: December 6, 1946, Preston, Lancashire, England.
Height: 5ft 11in.   *Weight:* 11st 0lb.
Right-handed batsman.
Teams: Lancashire and England.

Haroon Rashid

Frank Hayes

Career Highlights
1973: Hit an unbeaten 106 in second
   innings of his Test debut, against
   West Indies at the Oval.
1974: Scored 187 against the Indian
   tourists at Manchester.
1977: Took 34 in an over from
   Malcolm Nash, playing against
   Glamorgan at Swansea.

Rarely has a batsman scored so disappointing at international level. Frank
Hayes was hailed as the new hope of
English cricket after his sensational
Test debut yet he totalled only 244
runs in 17 innings. Perhaps unluckily
all his nine Tests were against the West
Indies. His talent was suppressed by
nerves. He captained Lancashire from
1978 to 1980.

Desmond Haynes

Born: February 15, 1956, St James,
   Barbados.
Height: 5ft 11½in.   *Weight:* 13st 7lb.
Right-handed batsman.
Teams: Barbados and West Indies.

Career Highlights
1980: Scored 184 against England at
   Lord's.

Desmond Haynes has been a patient
and assured opening partner to Gordon Greenidge for West Indies. He
first won a Test place against Australia
at Port of Spain in 1978 and scored
50s in each of his first three innings.
His rocklike effort against England in
1980 occupied eight and a quarter
hours.
   Although he is the more subdued
partner on the field when opening with
Gordon Greenidge, also a colleague in
the Barbados team, Haynes is a flam-
boyant character who epitomises West
Indian *joie de vivre.* He appeared for
Scotland in the 1983 Benson and
Hedges Cup, and became only the
fourth man to be given out 'handled
the ball' in Test cricket, when he was
dismissed against India in Bombay in
1983.

Desmond Haynes

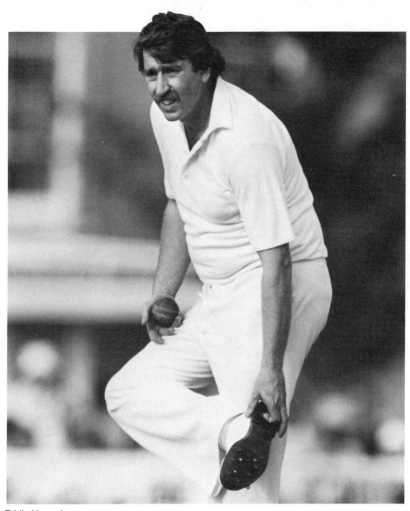

Eddie Hemmings

Eddie Hemmings

Born: February 20, 1949, Leamington
    Spa, Warwickshire, England.
Height: 5ft 10in.   *Weight:* 13st 0lb.
Right-arm   off-spin   bowler,   right-
    handed batsman.
Teams: Warwickshire, Nottinghamshire
and England.

Career Highlights
1982: Took all ten wickets for an Inter-
    national XI *v* West Indies XI,
    Kingston, Jamaica.

Eddie Hemmings began his career as a
medium-paced bowler with Warwickshire in 1966. He was not capped until

1974 and by the time he moved to Nottinghamshire in 1979 he had begun to blossom as a spin bowler. His 90 wickets in 1981 helped his new county win the Championship for the first time in 52 years. After 16 years in the game, he hit his maiden first class century – 127 not out against Yorkshire at Worksop in 1982.

He won his first cap as a 33-year-old *v* Pakistan in 1982, and went on England's tour of Australia and New Zealand the following winter.

His 12 wickets for England (in five Tests) proved rather costly at an average of 46.50, although in January 1983 against Australia at Sydney he failed by only five runs to score a Test match century. He recorded his best bowling of 7 for 23 against Lancashire at Trent Bridge in the summer of 1983.

in the winter of 1971-72, when the former electricity board worker got a job as a labourer, to make himself fitter and stronger, especially around the chest and shoulders. But, he received scant publicity for taking eight for 50 against Nottinghamshire that season – there was a newspaper strike the next morning!

His perfect action and height, enabling him to extract plenty of bounce from his medium-paced deliveries have helped him chalk up 87 wickets from Tests. He is currently banned from England duty for joining the 1982 unofficial tour to South Africa. After 12 years service to Derbyshire, he moved to Notts in 1982 and in 1983 was again well to the fore of the first class averages with 66 wickets.

Mike Hendrick

Born: October 22, 1948, Darley Dale, Derbyshire, England.
Height: 6ft 3in.   *Weight:* 14st 3lb.
Right-arm fast medium bowler.
Teams: Derbyshire, Nottinghamshire and England.

Career Highlights
1974: Entered Test Cricket and recorded best figures of four for 28 in his third match – against India at Birmingham.
1978-79: Played a valuable role in England's retention of the Ashes in Australia with 19 wickets at an average of 15.73 runs each.
1980: Took a hat trick for Derbyshire against the West Indians at Derby.

Mike Hendrick worked hard to make himself one of the best new ball bowlers in English cricket. He struggled to fulfil his potential until his mid-twenties. The turning point came

Graeme Hick

Born: May 23, 1966, Rhodesia.
Height: 6ft 2½in.   *Weight:* 13st 3lb.

Graeme Hick

Right-handed batsman, right-arm off spin bowler.
Team: Zimbabwe.

Career Highlights
1983: Test debut for Zimbabwe.

A schoolboy who forced his way into the Zimbabwe team against Young West Indies tourists in 1983, he hit an unbeaten 212 for Prince Edward High School one day, and another century for his club, Old Hararians, the next. He is a slip fielder who took three catches in his debut game for Zimbabwe.

Andrew Hilditch

Born: May 20, 1956, Adelaide, South Australia, Australia.
Height: 5ft 11in.   *Weight:* 11st 12lb.
Right-handed batsman.
Teams: New South Wales, South Australia and Australia.

Career Highlights
1978: Appointed captain of New South Wales at only 21.
1979: Vice-captain of Australia's World Cup team.

Solicitor Andrew Hilditch played nine Tests for Australia when they were weakened by the exodus of players to World Series Cricket and he scored 452 runs. However, his career then regressed and he moved to South Australia. His 109 for his new state against Tasmania in Adelaide, 1983, was only the second century of his career.

His place in the record books was assured when he became only the second batsman in Test history to be given out 'handled the ball' – this was against Pakistan at Perth in 1979. Andrew is the son-in-law of former Australian captain Bobby Simpson.

Tom Hogan

Born: September 23, 1956, Merredin, Perth, Western Australia.
Height: 6ft 1in.   *Weight:* 12st 9lb.
Slow left-arm bowler.
Teams: Western Australia and Australia.

Career Highlights
1983: Captured five for 66 on his Test debut, against Sri Lanka at Kandy.

Tom Hogan was picked for Australia after only two seasons of first class cricket, getting off to a good start against weak opposition in Sri Lanka. He was the spin bowler in the Australian World Cup side of 1983, bowling adequately in a disappointing team.

Tom has been coached in Western Australia by the former England left-arm spin bowler, Tony Lock, who now lives down under. The pick of his early performances was his six for 91 against eventual Sheffield Shield champions, New South Wales, at Sydney, 1982.

Rodney Hogg

Born: March 5, 1951, Melbourne, Victoria, Australia.
Height: 6ft 0in.   *Weight:* 12st 10lb.
Right-arm fast bowler.
Teams: Victoria, South Australia and Australia.

Career Highlights
1978-79: Claimed 41 wickets in his first Test series, against England.

Rodney Hogg made his mark at international level at the comparatively late age, for a fast bowler, of 27 – while the likes of Lillee and Thomson were away playing for Kerry Packer. His 41 wickets were a record for a debutant and have been bettered only by Jim Laker,

Sydney Barnes, Clarrie Grimmett and Terry Alderman. Hogg took 10 wickets in both the Perth and Melbourne Tests.

He has not produced quite such devastating form since, although in 1983 against Pakistan he passed 100 wickets in his 28th Test. He was Australia's leading bowler (with nine victims) during their disastrous World Cup that year.

Michael Holding

Born: February 16, 1954, St Andrew, Kingston, Jamaica.
Height: 6ft 3in.   *Weight:* 12st 12lb.
Right-arm fast bowler.
Teams: Jamaica, Lancashire, Tasmania, Derbyshire and West Indies.

Career Highlights
1976: Set West Indian record when he took 14 wickets in a Test match – *v* England at the Oval.
1983: Passed 150 wickets after 36 Tests.

Within a year of his Test debut for West Indies against Australia at Brisbane in late 1975, Michael Holding was being hailed as the fastest bowler in the world. Yet his selection for that tour was seen in some quarters as a gamble. He first played for Jamaica in 1972-73 and, although he three times clean bowled Ian Redpath (touring with the Australians) that season he did not produce the figures to press his international claims.

When he got to Australia, some of his team mates had not seen him bowl for two years and they were astonished at the pace he showed in the first game. He won the second Test for West Indies, but was then injured and that remained their only victory of a

Michael Holding

disastrous series.

English spectators had their first view of the graceful, lithe Holding (a former quarter miler) in 1976. He took five for 17 to bowl England out for 71 on a bad wicket at Manchester. Then in the final Test he produced one of the most remarkable bowling feats of modern times. The Oval pitch was dead, yet he took eight for 92 and six for 57 to give West Indies a 231 runs win.

Holding, a computer programmer, is mild-mannered off the field and his petulant display at Dunedin in the first Test of 1980 against New Zealand surprised most observers. He kicked down the stumps after an appeal for a catch off his bowling was rejected.

He had one season for Lancashire in 1981, topping their bowling averages, and in 1983 joined Derbyshire on a two-year contract.

David Hookes

David Hookes

Born: May 3, 1955, Mile End,
   Adelaide, South Australia, Australia.
Height: 6ft 0in.   *Weight:* 13st 0lb.
Left-handed batsman.
Teams: South Australia and Australia.

Career Highlights
1976-77: Five centuries in six innings
   for South Australia.
1982: Hit a hundred off only 34 balls
   against Victoria at Adelaide. His 107
   was his second century of that match.

Perhaps the most gifted of the new
breed of Australian batsmen, but also
among the most impetuous. His
tremendous run of form in 1976-77
earned him a place in the Centenary
Test against England – and he thrilled
the huge crowd at Melbourne by hitting five successive fours off the bowling of England captain Tony Greig.

He struggled to establish himself in
the Test team after two years with
Kerry Packer's World Series. But he
led South Australia to the Sheffield
Shield in 1981-82 – and the following
season had another magic run with the
bat. He totalled 1,501 – joining Bradman, Greg Chappell and Ponsford as
the only batsmen to pass 1,500. He
was a consistent, if not prolific, member of the Ashes winning team and
after 14 Tests scored his maiden century – against Sri Lanka at Kandy in
1983.

Just when it seemed Hookes's
future was finally mapped out – he was
appointed vice-captain of Australia's
1983 World Cup team – matters started to go awry. The Cup campaign was
a disaster and Hookes was openly criti-
cal of captain Kim Hughes, his opi-
nions costing him a fine of 1,200
Australian dollars and he was unable to
get in the Test team at the start of the
1983-84 series against Pakistan.

David Houghton

Born: June 23, 1957, Salisbury,
   Rhodesia.
Height: 5ft 10in.   *Weight:* 12st 12lb.
Wicket-keeper, right-handed batsman.
Teams: Rhodesia and Zimbabwe.

Career Highlights
1982: Three man of the match awards
   when Zimbabwe won the ICC
   Trophy.

David Houghton produced some sterl-
ing innings for Zimbabwe in the 1983
World Cup, including 84 against Australia and 54 against West Indies. He
was goalkeeper for the national hockey
team for several seasons.

Geoff Howarth MBE

Born: March 29, 1951, Auckland, New
   Zealand.
Height: 5ft 11in.   *Weight:* 12st 0lb.
Right-handed batsman, off-spin
   bowler.
Teams: Auckland, Northern Districts,
   Surrey and New Zealand.

Career Highlights
1978: Scored 122 and 102 for New
   Zealand *v* England in Auckland.
1979-80: In New Zealand, led his
   country to 1-0 win over West Indies
   and captained Northern Districts to
   Shell Trophy and Cup double.

Geoff Howarth has been the successful
captain of New Zealand since 1980. In
fact, by 1983 he had led his country in
half of the 34 Tests he had played. He
has also proved a resourceful top order
batsman, thriving on the responsibility
of captaincy.

However, it took a long time for his
career to take off. He joined the Surrey
ground staff in 1969, making his debut
two years later. But he did not repre-

sent a New Zealand provincial side until 1972-73, playing a season with Auckland before switching to Northern Districts.

His captaincy won much praise in England in 1983. Although the four-match series was lost 3-1, New Zealand's victory at Leeds was their first in a Test in England.

His elder brother, Hedley, a left-arm spin bowler, played 30 Tests.

Geoff Howarth

Kim Hughes batting.

Kim Hughes

Born: January 26, 1954, Margaret River, Western Australia, Australia.
Height: 5ft 11½in.　*Weight:* 12st 4lb.
Right-handed batsman.
Teams: Western Australia and Australia.

Career Highlights
1981: Hit record score for an

Australian against India with 213 at Adelaide.

1982-83: Topped Australia's batting against England with 469 runs, average 67.

Kim Hughes first captained Australia at 25, when he took over from the injured Graham Yallop against Pakistan, at the end of the 1978-79 season.

He was impressive enough for the selectors to retain him for that year's World Cup and a subsequent tour to India, but once the Kerry Packer circus was disbanded Australia preferred Greg Chappell (when available) as their leader.

Hughes has been unfortunate to be in charge for the last two World Cups, when Australia have performed well below their capabilities, and in Pakistan in 1982, when they were hammered by Imran Khan. It is often said that Hughes was resented by other senior players, which has puzzled most outsiders, who see him as an intelligent and modest cricketer and one of the most watchable batsmen in the world. However, he finally appeared to assert himself in the 1983-84 Australian season, when he had a full-strength side under him for the return series against Pakistan and led them to a 2-0 victory.

Hughes's talent for batting was obvious from an early age ... he was playing senior club cricket in Perth at 15. He was impatient for a chance at State level and when he failed to make the Western Australia team by the age

of 19 he moved to Adelaide. But he fared no better there, moved back to Perth, and the following season was given his opportunity at first class level. He had a point to prove after waiting for his first game, and he scored 119 and 60 against New South Wales.

Two years later, in 1977, he made his Test debut during the tour of England. He declined to join World Series Cricket and established himself while the 'big guns' were away firing for Kerry Packer. He has scored more than 4,000 runs for his country. He was the star of an otherwise dreary Centenary Test at Lords in 1980, when he made 117 and 84, and, in the 1980-81 season, he led Western Australia to the Sheffield Shield.

Imran Khan

Imran Khan

Born: November 25, 1952, Lahore,
Pakistan.
Height: 6ft 0in.   *Weight:* 12st 2lb.
Right-arm fast bowler, right-handed
batsman.
Teams: Lahore, PIA, Worcestershire,
Sussex and Pakistan.

Career Highlights
1977: Spearheaded Pakistan's first win
in Australia with 12 wickets in the
match at Sydney.
1982: At Lord's, led his country to
their first win for 28 years against
England. Claimed 40 wickets in the
1982-83 series against India,
including eight for 60 at Karachi,
which took him past 200.

Imran Khan took over the captaincy of
Pakistan in 1982, after a players'
rebellion against Javed Miandad. It
soon became obvious that the choice,
seen at the time as a compromise, was
inspired. Imran, who during his late
twenties had developed into one of the
game's fastest bowlers, also emerged
as a more responsible batsman. He led
by example, and showed a maturity
and tactical awareness which surprised
even some of his close colleagues.

His explosive, fast bowling action and
his handsome athleticism projected an
image which attracted maximum
publicity. There was much interest in
his rivalry with Ian Botham, and with
India's Kapil Dev also playing Test
cricket in England that summer, there
was an unofficial contest for the title of
the world's greatest all-rounder. All
three played so well that there seemed
nothing to choose between them, but
Imran stated his case firmly in the
ensuing year.

He captained Pakistan to an
emphatic 3-0 win over Australia, he
next took 40 wickets and averaged 61

with the bat in the crushing of India,
and he finished top of Pakistan's batting averages in the 1983 World Cup,
when he was unable to bowl because of
a stress fracture to his left shin. There
was just time before the English
season ended for him to take a hat
trick and six for six for Sussex against
Warwickshire and to score 94 and 64 in
the same match.

Injury prevented his bowling in the
1983-84 series against Australia, when
he played the last two Tests as a
batsman.

It is a popular misconception that
Imran rose from poverty in Pakistan.
In fact, his father was a landowner and
Imran, whose cousins Javed Burki and
Majid Khan also captained Pakistan,
comes from the proud Pathan stock
which also produces the world's top
squash players. He made his Test
debut as an 18-year-old medium paced
bowler in England, in 1971, while still
a schoolboy. His first English county
was Worcestershire, but after three
years at Oxford (1973-75), where he
gained an honours degree in politics
and economics, he moved to Sussex.

In a Test match against New Zealand
at Karachi in 1976, Imran was banned
from bowling by the umpires for persistent short-pitched deliveries. He
was one of the Packer pirates and it
was this phase of his career, when he
changed his action and was helped by
Mike Procter and John Snow, that saw
his bowling improve dramatically. He
has a particularly devastating late in-
swinger, and is Pakistan's highest
wicket-taker in Tests.

Bachelor Imran's personal life has
been a hot topic of speculation for
gossip columnists. He enjoys Western
nightlife, but is teetotal, drinking three
and a half pints of milk a day! He has
said that, as a devout Muslim, he will
accept his parents' choice of a bride.

John Inverarity

Born: January 1, 1944, Perth, Western
Australia, Australia.
Height: 6ft 2in.   *Weight:* 12st 0lb.
Right-handed batsman, left-arm spin
bowler.
Teams: Western Australia, South
Australia and Australia.

Career Highlights
1968-72: Six Tests, five *v* England.
1978: Scored 187 for Western
Australia *v* New South Wales.
1983: Overtook Sir Donald Bradman's
record aggregate of 8,926 runs in the
Sheffield Shield.

John Inverarity is the longest serving
player in Australian state cricket, having made his debut in the 1962-63
season. He was not a great success as a
Test batsman, with a top score of only
56, achieved in difficult conditions
against England at the Oval, 1968. But
he was an outstanding captain of a
talented Western Australia side in the
1970s. A school teacher, he has played
the latter part of his career with South
Australia, helping them win the Sheffield Shield in 1981-82 with 30 wickets
in his secondary role of left arm spin
bowler. Although Inverarity beat Bradman's Shield record aggregate of runs
he needed 258 innings compared to
the Don's 96.

Iqbal Qasim

Born: August 6, 1953, Karachi,
Pakistan.
Height: 5ft 6in.   *Weight:* 10st 6lb.
Left-arm spin bowler.
Teams: Karachi, Sind, National Bank
and Pakistan.

Career Highlights
1980: Seven for 49 for Pakistan against
Australia, Karachi.

Iqbal Qasim has taken 115 wickets in
37 Tests since his debut in 1976. It
seemed at one time that he might
strike up a brilliant spin partnership
with Abdul Qadir, but they have rarely
been on song together and the Pakistan selectors have usually seen one or
the other as expendable. Qasim had
his moment, however, against Australia in 1980. His 11 wickets in the
match brought Pakistan victory – and
they held on to take the three-match
series 1-0.

On the domestic front, Qasim picked up 41 wickets in helping National
Bank win the Quaid-e-Azam Trophy in
1981-82.

Javed Miandad

Born: June 6, 1957, Karachi, Pakistan.
Height: 5ft 9in.   *Weight:* 11st 7lb.
Right-handed batsman, leg-spin
bowler.
Teams: Karachi, Sind, Habib Bank,
Sussex, Glamorgan and Pakistan.

Career Highlights
1976: Became only the second
Pakistani to score a century in his
first Test innings with 163 against
New Zealand at Lahore, in the
process setting his country's best
fifth wicket stand with Asif Iqbal of
281. In same series, and in his third
Test, Javed made 206 at Karachi and
at 19 years and 141 days was
youngest double centurion in Tests.
1983: Javed and Mudassar Nazar
equalled world Test record stand for
any wicket, when they put on 451
against India at Hyderabad
(matching Bradman and Ponsford at
the Oval in 1934). Javed's share was
an unbeaten 280, second highest
innings ever for Pakistan.

Javed   Miandad's   rare   talent   was

Javed Miandad

obvious from the match in 1974-75, when he scored 311 for Karachi Whites against National Bank as a 17-year-old. He has maintained his promise to become one of the most free-scoring batsmen in world cricket, although his career has not been without controversy. He has shown a hot temper on the field. He was involved in a flare up with Dennis Lillee on the 1981-82 tour to Australia, and the image of the game was done no good by the sight of Javed, bat raised above his head, squaring up to the Australian fast bowler. After this series there was a players' revolt in the Pakistani dressing room and Javed, who had been captain in 13 Tests, made way for Imran Khan.

He first played in English county cricket for Sussex but when they became overloaded with foreign players he switched to Glamorgan. He immediately established a double record for the county by scoring 2,083 runs and eight centuries in his first season.

Recently, Javed and Zaheer Abbas have been running neck and neck, with over 4,000 runs apiece, as Pakistan's highest-ever Test scorers. But with age on his side, Javed is sure to have this record to himself eventually.

Bernard Julien
Born: March 13, 1950, Carenage, Trinidad.
Height: 5ft 11in.   *Weight:* 12st 0lb.
Right-handed batsman, left-arm fast-medium or spin bowler.
Teams: Trinidad and Tobago, Kent and West Indies.

Career Highlights
1973: A brilliant 121 off only 127 balls for West Indies against England at Lord's. This was his maiden first

Alvin Kallicharran

class century.
1982: Took nine for 97 for Trinidad and Tobago *v* Jamaica at Port of Spain.

During the mid-seventies, Bernard Julien threatened to become one of cricket's major figures. But, partly because of his carefree attitude to life, he was never able to sustain the promise of his early international career when, in successive series away and at home against England, he scored over 400 runs and took 23 wickets in eight games.

He signed for the West Indian rebels who toured South Africa in 1983.

Alvin Kallicharran

Born: March 21, 1949, Paidama, British Guiana.
Height: 5ft 4in.   *Weight:* 9st 7lb.
Left-handed batsman, occasional right-arm off spin bowler.
Teams: Guyana, Warwickshire, Queensland, Transvaal and West Indies.

Career Highlights
1972: Scored a century in each of his first two Test innings, both against New Zealand at Georgetown and Port of Spain.
1982: Shared a record fourth wicket stand for all English counties of 470 with Geoff Humpage, Warwickshire against Lancashire at Southport, when Kallicharran's total for the season was 2,120.
1983: Hit 243 not out *v* Glamorgan at Birmingham.

Alvin Kallicharran, nine times captain of the West Indies, caused a furore when he accepted £20,000 a season to coach and play in South Africa in the

1981-82 season. He was banned from playing again for his country, but the next season he was joined by a party of West Indians for an unofficial tour of the land of apartheid.

Kallicharran's momentous change of course seems to have precipitated a resurgence of his very best form as a left-handed batsman, who can hit the ball astonishingly hard considering his slight build. In his first season in South Africa he hit 484 runs in 10 innings for Transvaal. He then returned to Warwickshire to enjoy his best season for them since he joined in 1971, with more than 2,000 runs and eight centuries, including three scores of over 200.

The hot streak continued into the 1982-83 South African season, where he not only hammered another 822 runs and averaged over 50, but helped Transvaal win the domestic treble of Currie Cup, Datsun Shield and the Benson and Hedges night series. Back in England in 1983, he improved his career best score to 243 not out, against Glamorgan at Birmingham.

'Kalli' was one of 11 children of a rice and coconut farmer in Guyana. Isaac Kallicharran captained Port Mourant, which has given Basil Butcher, among several others, to the West Indies team. But it was Kallicharran's Uncle Ramjee, a Port Mourant shopkeeper, who most encouraged the youngster's interest in cricket by paying his club fees. At 16, Kallicharran became the youngest to play for Guyana in the Shell Shield and was indebted to a rum manufacturer who provided him with his kit and a job.

His promise drew interest from English counties before he had made the West Indies team and, but for a postal strike which held up negotiations, he might have joined Glamorgan in 1971. However, Warwickshire became his county when Alan Smith jetted out to the Caribbean. With fellow West Indian Rohan Kanhai, plus England players Mike Smith, Dennis Amiss and John Jameson, he became a member of the strongest batting line-up in the county game.

Lalith Kaluperuma

Born: June 25, 1949, Colombo, Ceylon.
Height: 5ft 11in.   *Weight:* 11st 12lb.
Right-arm off spin bowler.
Teams: Bloomfield and Sri Lanka.

Career Highlights
1982: Two Tests for Sri Lanka.

He played two Tests against England and Pakistan in 1982, before being banned from international cricket for 25 years after joining the unofficial tour to South Africa.

Kapil Dev

Born: January 1, 1959, Chandigarh, India.
Height: 6ft 0in.   *Weight:* 11st 9lb.
Right-handed batsman, right-arm fast bowler.
Teams: Haryana, Northamptonshire, Worcestershire and India.

Career Highlights
1983: Captained India to victory in World Cup competition, setting a record individual score for competition with 175 not out against Zimbabwe. Earlier that year against West Indies beat Ian Botham's record as youngest Test player to complete Test double of 2,000 runs and 200 wickets. He was 24 years and 68 days (but needed 50 Tests compared to Botham's 42).

No star of India ever shone brighter on the cricket field than Kapil Dev, who led his team to an astonishing World Cup triumph in 1983 with victory in the final over twice-champions West Indies. He was India's captain, chief runmaker (303 from eight innings) and also took 12 wickets. In the preliminary stages, India's position looked irretrievable at Tunbridge Wells, when no-hopers Zimbabwe reduced them to 17 for five. But Kapil's 175 not out (six 6s and sixteen 4s) set them on their way to an eventual 31 runs victory.

Kapil returned to India a national hero – and yet might have played for Pakistan had his parents not emigrated from Rawalpindi to Chandigarh, where the family set up a building and timber business, which has prospered to the extent that Kapil does not need to play cricket for a living. He plays for fun, and it shows as at Lord's in 1982, when he was on course for the fastest-ever Test century before he was out for 89 off 55 balls against England.

The responsibility that Kapil carries for his country shows no sign yet of wearing him down. Against West Indies in October 1983 at Ahmedabad he took nine for 83, only the third time an Indian has taken nine wickets in an innings.

He made his debut as a 16-year-old for Haryana (there they call him the Hurricane) and took six for 39 against Punjab, having switched to seam bowling after starting out as a spinner.

He joined Worcestershire on a two-year contract in 1984.

Collis King

Born: June 11, 1951, St Patrick's, Barbados.
Height: 6ft 1in.   *Weight:* 12st 2lb.
Right-handed batsman and medium-paced bowler.

Kapil Dev

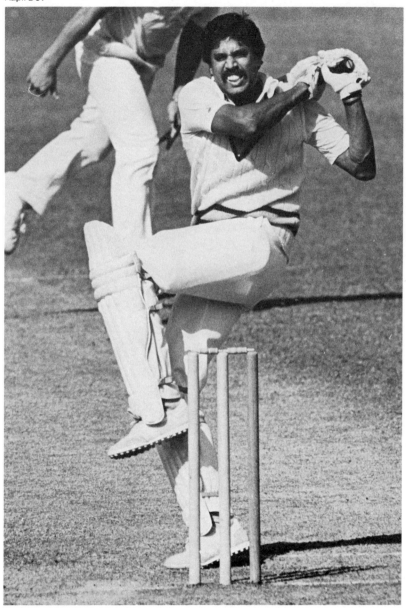

Collis King

Team: West Indies.
Career Highlights
1979: Scored 86 off only 66 balls for
  West Indies against England in
  World Cup.

There are not many fiercer hitters of
the ball than Collis King, whose
scorching innings in the 1979 World
Cup final revived West Indies after
England had reduced them to 99 for
four. On his first tour of England in
1976, he hit six centuries, but was disappointing when playing for
Glamorgan in 1977. He joined the
rebel tour of South Africa in 1983,
scoring a typically thunderous century
(off 115 balls with a six and 15 fours) in
the second four-day international at
Johannesburg.

Syed Kirmani

Born: December 29, 1949, Madras,
   India.
Height: 5ft 5½in.   *Weight:* 9st 4lb.
Wicket-keeper, right-handed batsman.
Teams: Karnataka and India.

Career Highlights
1976: Equalled the Test record of six
   victims in an innings (five caught and
   one stumped), in his second match
   for India, against New Zealand at
   Christchurch.

Syed Kirmani first toured England
with India in 1971, but had to wait five
years (due to the excellence of Farokh
Engineer), before he made his Test

Syed Kirmani

debut against New Zealand. Once
Engineer retired, Kirmani established
himself as a top-quality keeper and an
adequate batsman at the highest level.
He was a member of India's 1983
World Cup winning side, and that year
passed 150 Test victims and 2,000
runs.

Kirti Azad

Kirti Azad

Born: January 2, 1959, Purnea, Bihar,
   India.
Height: 5ft 11in.   *Weight:* 12st 2lb.
Right-handed batsman and off-spin
   bowler.
Teams: Delhi and India.

Career Highlights
1983: Member of Indian team which
   won World Cup.

Kirti, the son of an Indian Government
minister, was a surprise choice for the
1983 World Cup. He made his Test
debut against New Zealand at
Wellington, in 1981, and also appeared
against England in 1981-82.

Alan Knott

Alan Knott

Born: April 6, 1946, Belvedere, Kent, England.
Height: 5ft 8in.   *Weight:* 10st 10lb.
Wicket-keeper and right-handed batsman.
Teams: Kent and England.

Career Highlights
1967: Took seven catches in debut Test for England against Pakistan at Nottingham.
1970-71: Claimed 24 dismissals in series against Australia; set England seventh wicket record *v* New Zealand of 71 with Peter Lever at Auckland; set England seventh wicket record *v* Pakistan of 159 with Peter Lever at Birmingham.
1973: Set England tenth wicket record *v* New Zealand of 59 with Norman Gifford at Nottingham.
1974: Set England sixth wicket record *v* West Indies of 163 with Tony Greig at Bridgetown.
1976: Became first wicket-keeper to complete 200 Test catches.
1977: Set England sixth wicket record *v* Australia of 215 with Geoff Boycott at Nottingham.
1981: Increased his Test aggregate of runs to 4,389, a record for any wicket-keeper. His total of 263 dismissals is the best for England.

Alan Knott, England's most successful wicket-keeper/batsman, was a more or less permanent fixture in the side from his debut in 1967, aged 21, until joining Kerry Packer's World Series Cricket ten years later. He had then established an England record of 65 consecutive appearances. He was recalled in 1980, and also in 1981 when he helped to win an Ashes series as he had in both 1970-71 and 1977. But his Test career was probably ended, when he was banned for three

years for going with the rebels to South Africa.

His former Kent and England captain Colin Cowdrey once said of Knott: *'He is the most gifted and dedicated cricketer one could ever wish to play with.'* Praise indeed from somone whose own career lasted a quarter of a century and included a record 114 Tests.

Knott's first wicket-keeping experience was in the hall of his home with his father Eric, who kept for the Belvedere club. They would take it in turns to stand behind the other and throw a ball against a wall. One kept wicket while the other played at the ball with a stump. This provided ideal practice at taking deflections!

Knott was picked for Kent Schools as a 14-year-old. Derek Underwood, Geoff Arnold and David Sadler, who was to become an England footballer, were also in that team. Knott, in short trousers, ventured into the dressing room and was asked by the team manager: *'What do you want, son?'* Knott replied: *'I have come to play.'*

Fitness-fanatic Knott was capped by Kent in 1965, aged 19, and in 1967 dismissed 98 batsmen. He scored 127 not out and 118 not out in the same match *v* Surrey at Maidstone in 1977. And he and schoolboy colleague Derek Underwood have been to the fore in Kent, winning the Championship in 1970, '77 (shared) and '78, the Gillette Cup in 1967 and '74, the Benson and Hedges Cup in 1973, '76, '78 and the Sunday League in 1972, '73, '76.

Bruce Laird

Born: November 21, 1951, Mount Lawley, Western Australia, Australia.
Height: 5ft 10in.   *Weight:* 11st 0lb.
Right-handed batsman.
Teams: Western Australia and Australia.

Madan Lal

Career Highlights
1976: 171 for Western Australia *v*
  Queensland at Brisbane.
1979: Scored 92 and 75 on Test debut
  v West Indies at Brisbane.

Opening batsman Bruce Laird was one of the few Australia players who joined Kerry Packer's World Series Cricket in 1977 without previous Test match experience, although he had been on the tour to England in 1975. However, he was undaunted by star company and scored three centuries in the super-Tests before resuming 'official' cricket in 1979. He was a consistent opening batsman for his country without reaching 100 in 21 Tests.

Madan Lal

Born: March 20, 1951, Amritsar, India.
Height: 5ft 10in.   *Weight:* 11st 7lb.
Right-arm fast medium bowler, right-
  handed batsman.
Teams: Delhi, Punjab and India.

Career Highlights
1978: Scored 223 for Delhi *v*
  Rajasthan, Ranj Trophy quarter-
  final.
1983: Member of India's victorious
  World Cup team taking three
  wickets in final *v* West Indies.

Madal Lal is a whole-hearted bowler who can also bat, although he is rarely devastating at Test level in either role. Nevertheless, he has served India well since his debut in 1974. He secured his country's victory in the home rubber against England in 1981-82 by taking five for 23 at Bombay.

Allan Lamb

Born: June 20, 1954, Langebaanweg,
  South Africa.
Height: 5ft 8in.   *Weight:* 12st 12lb.
Right-handed batsman.

Teams: Western Province, Northants and England.

Career Highlights
1980: Topped the English averages with 1,797 runs at an average of 66.55.
1981: Scored 2,049 runs in season.
1982: Scored 107 in his third Test match against India at the Oval.
1983: Took his aggregate to over 1,000 in his 15th Test. Equalled England record for catches in a Test match by a non-wicket-keeper with six against New Zealand at Lord's in August.

Allan Lamb, a South African whose parents are from London, was an automatic choice for England as soon as he qualified in 1982. He came to England in 1977 and joined Northants the following season. While arguments continue to rage about the qualification rules which allow an increasing number of foreigners to play for England, there is no doubting Lamb's ability.

In six seasons in his adopted country, he has scored more than 9,000 runs. Back home in South Africa, where he made his debut for Western Province as an 18-year-old in the 1972-73 Currie Cup, he has proved just as run-hungry. He missed two seasons in the mid-seventies to do his national service with the South African Air Force, but between 1977 and 1982 topped 3,000 runs in the shorter season there.

He is an attacking batsman who says: *'My objective is to look for runs off every ball. I dislike leaving the bad ball, such as the wide or a long hop, as some batsmen do.'*

He has appeared in two Cup finals at Lord's for Northants, helping them win the Benson and Hedges in 1980. On each occasion he has taken his score into the 70s. *'I thrive before a large crowd. It excites and challenges me and Lord's is the perfect setting,'* he says. A born winner, in 1981-82 he played his part in Western Province's Currie Cup and Datsun Shield double success.

One of his hobbies is collecting antiques. His brother-in-law is Tony Bucknall, the former England rugby union player.

Allan Lamb

Wayne Larkins

Born: November 22, 1953, Roxton,
  Bedfordshire, England.
Height: 5ft 11in.   *Weight:* 12st 0lb.
Right-handed batsman and right-arm
  medium-paced bowler.
Teams: Northants, Eastern Province
  and England.

Career Highlights
1976: Played in the Northants team
  which won the Gillette Cup.
1980: Member of the Northants team
  which won the Benson and Hedges
  Cup. Set Northants second wicket
  record of 322, with Richard Williams
  against Leicestershire, at Leicester.
  Took a hat trick in Benson and
  Hedges Cup match against
  Combined Universities.
1983: Hit a career best (and highest of
  the English season), 252, for
  Northants versus Glamorgan at
  Cardiff in August, with a century
  before lunch and another between
  lunch and tea.

Larkins is a forcing opener with
Northants, lost to England for three
years because of his participation in
the 1982 rebel tour to South Africa.
Geoff Boycott apart, Larkins has been
the most consistent English opener on
the county scene during the 1980s,
with a total of 6,954 runs in four
seasons. But in 11 Test innings between 1979 and 1981 he managed only
176. An occasional medium-paced
bowler, he had limited success playing
for Eastern Province in the 1982-83
Currie Cup.

Geoff Lawson

Born: December 7, 1957, Wagga
  Wagga, New South Wales, Australia.
Height: 6ft 4½in.   *Weight:* 12st 4lb.
Right-arm fast bowler.

Geoff Lawson

Teams: New South Wales, Lancashire
  and Australia.

Career Highlights
1982: His 34 wickets against England
  helped Australia win back the Ashes.

Had Geoff Lawson remained fit during
his first tour of England in 1980, then
the 'Botham series' might well have
had a different result. He looked the
most hostile bowler on either side
when taking seven for 81 at Lord's
(only Bob Massie has done better at
cricket's headquarters for Australia),
but missed the last of the six-Test
series with a back injury.

Lawson, who studied optometry at
New South Wales University, reached
peak form again in the 1982-83 season.
Besides undermining the English
batsmen, he was in great form for his
state, helping New South Wales win
the Sheffield Shield for the first time in
17 years with 65 wickets.

He played League cricket in
England in 1979, taking 94 wickets for
Heywood and making one appearance
(against Cambridge University) for
Lancashire.

Warren Lees

Born: March 19, 1952, Dunedin, New
  Zealand.
Height: 5ft 10½in.   *Weight:* 12st 3lb.
Wicket-keeper and right-handed
batsman.
Teams: Otago and New Zealand.

Career Highlights
1976: Hit 152 against Pakistan at
  Karachi, sharing a New Zealand
  seventh wicket record against all
  countries of 186 with Richard
  Hadlee.
1983: Claimed his 50th Test victim
  against Sri Lanka at Wellington.

Warren Lees, a secondary school
teacher, succeeded the late Ken
Wadsworth as New Zealand's wicket-
keeper in 1976. Although he played in
the 1983 World Cup, he was replaced
by Ian Smith for two of the Tests
against England.

John Lever

Born: February 24, 1949, Stepney,
  London, England.
Height: 6ft 0in.   *Weight:* 13st 0lb.
Left-arm fast medium bowler.
Teams: Essex, Natal and England.

Career Highlights
1976: Took seven for 46 on Test debut
  v India in Delhi in December.
1979: Took 106 wickets to help Essex
  win Championship. Recorded best
  figures of eight for 49 *v* Warwickshire
  at Birmingham.
1983: Took 106 wickets to help Essex
  win Championship again.

John Lever went on five England tours
between 1976 and 1982 before throw-
ing in his lot with the rebel tour to
South Africa. He was a controversial
match-winner in his first Test, taking

10 wickets against India at Delhi. He
swung the ball to such an extent that
there were suggestions, later dis-
proved, that it had been shined with
Vaseline. He went on to take 67 wickets in 20 games for England.

He is noted for his stamina and
athleticism in the field. And he showed
his courage in 1983 when he returned
from a mid-season stomach operation
to play a significant role in Essex's winning of the County Championship.

John Lever

Dennis Lillee MBE

Born: July 18, 1949, Subiaco, Western
  Australia, Australia.
Height: 6ft 0in.   *Weight:* 13st 10lb.
Right-arm fast bowler.
Teams: Western Australia and
  Australia.

Career Highlights
1977: Won Centenary Test with 11
  victims against England.
1981: Became highest wicket-taker in

Test history at Melbourne, when passed previous best career total of 309 set by the West Indian spinner, Lance Gibbs. Set a record for an Australian in England with 39 wickets in the six-Test series.

1983-84: Against Pakistan he improved his record to 355 wickets before retiring from Tests.

This great fast bowler has shown not only skill and strength, but also the courage to rebuild his career when it seemed cut off at its peak by a stress fracture in his back. Even after a demoralising World Cup in 1983, he was back yet again at the age of 34 as part of Australia's strike force against Pakistan.

Lillee made his Australia debut, having previously toured with a B team to New Zealand, in the 1970-71 series against England, when wicket-keeper Rod Marsh and batsman Greg Chappell were also introduced to the international scene. Marsh, in fact, was to appear behind the stumps in every Test Lillee played until his 65th, against Sri Lanka at Kandy, in 1983.

By the time Lillee made his first tour of England in 1972, he had already gained experience of the conditions by playing a season with Haslingden in the Lancashire League. *'That was a turning point in my career,'* he said. *'It forced me to become more accurate rather than merely thump the ball down as fast as possible.'* Lillee's style was built on a classical fast bowler's action (he had received advice from Ray Lindall as a teenager) and in the 1972 series he set a record of 31 wickets by an Australian in England which stood for nine years.

However, he incurred his back injury in the West Indies in 1973 and he needed a long rest before teaming up with Jeff Thomson to terrorise

Dennis Lillee (right)

England in 1974-75, when the fearsome duo shared 58 wickets. Lillee has delighted in plaguing Australia's oldest enemy; he has claimed a record 167 victims in Tests with England.

He played two seasons with World Series Cricket, but on his return to the established game he showed little loss of hostility. However, he caused an outcry at the Perth Test during England's tour of 1979-80, when he used an aluminium bat, which the umpires ordered him to change for a

wooden one. And again at Perth, against Pakistan, two years later he was involved in a scuffle with Javed Miandad, aiming a kick at him and the then Pakistan captain raising his bat at the bowler in retaliation.

Lillee was magnificent during Australia's losing tour of England in 1981, compensating for his lessening pace by using all his experience as a swing and seam bowler. However, he and Marsh met with widespread disapproval when they revealed they had bet at 500-1 on Australia to lose the Leeds Test (and lose they did, for the two Aussies to pick up profits of £5,000).

Lillee's burning determination was never better demonstrated than against West Indies at Melbourne in the Christmas Test of 1981, when he went into the match needing five wickets to beat Lance Gibbs record total of 309. There was no doubt who was deserving of the record, when Lillee produced his best-ever Test match return of seven for 83!

Clive Lloyd

Clive Lloyd

Born: August 31, 1944, Georgetown,
British Guiana.
Height: 6ft 4½in.   *Weight:* 14st 0lb.
Left-handed batsman, right-arm
medium-paced bowler.
Teams: Guyana, Lancashire and West
Indies.

Career Highlights
1972: Scored 126 against
Warwickshire at Lord's, when
Lancashire won Gilette Cup for third
year running.
1975: Captained victorious World Cup
team.
1976: His 201 not out in 120 minutes
for the West Indians *v* Glamorgan
equalled Gilbert Jessop's record for
the fastest double century in first
class cricket.
1979: Second World Cup victory as
captain.
1983: Passed 6,000 Test runs and
enjoyed his best series with 671 runs
against India.

The hulking frame of Clive Lloyd is
one of the most recognisable – and
popular – sights in cricket. His merci-
less, left-handed batting has routed all
varieties of attacks over the past two
decades. In his prime, his fielding in
the covers, which he guarded with an
inimitable, loping stride, earned him
the nickname of Supercat. When knee
trouble slowed him down, at one stage
threatening to end his career, he
moved to the slips, from whence he has
directed the operations of his redoubt-
able fast bowlers.

Clive, a cousin of Lance Gibbs,
developed his skill with the bat as a
boy in the back streets of British
Guiana (as it then was), with his
brother and four sisters. He was forced
to wear glasses after his eyesight was
damaged when he broke up a fight as a

12-year-old, but this did not deter him. Three seasons after his first class debut, he was in the Test team (on the 1966-67 tour to India). England first encountered him on their trip to the Caribbean the next year, when Lloyd introduced himself in the first Test with 118. In 1968, Lancashire, having failed to sign Sobers, took on Lloyd instead, and his influence on them was enormous. He revels in the one-day game and he helped them win four Gillette Cup finals in the seventies. Three times he played match-winning innings, the outstanding one being 126 against Warwickshire in 1972. His reputation as a winner was emphasised when Guyana won the West Indies' domestic competition, the Shell Shield, in 1973 and '75.

Clive himself assumed captaincy responsibilities when he took over the West Indies' helm from Rohan Kanhai in November 1974 and celebrated at the expense of the Indians. He hit 636 runs in a five-match series, including his Test best of 242 not out at Bombay. He has captained West Indies in more than 50 Tests – a record for any country.

There has followed a decade of success, save only for the heavy defeat by the Australians in 1975-76 and a hiccup against New Zealand in 1979-80. In the one-day game, Lloyd and his men seemed invincible until the World Cup was snatched from them by India in 1983.

Lloyd suffered a bad hamstring injury, which forced him to hobble out of the fourth Test and miss the fifth against England in 1980. He recovered to kill talk that his career was over. Even in his 40th year he showed, with a calming 103 in the oppressive heat of Delhi, that he remained a major Test batsman and one of the best ever big occasion players.

Gus Logie

Born: September 28, 1960, Trinidad.
Height: 5ft 4in.   *Weight:* 9st 0lb.
Right-handed batsman.
Teams: Trinidad & Tobago and West
  Indies.

Career Highlights
1983: 130 in his fourth Test
  appearance against India.

Augustine Logie came into the West
Indies team in 1983 after several of
their stars had 'defected' to South
Africa. He had enjoyed three successful seasons with Trinidad and Tobago
in the Shell Shield, making 171 against
Jamaica at Port of Spain in 1982. He
did not get into the West Indies 1983
World Cup team, but was picked later
in the year for the tour of India.

Gus Logie

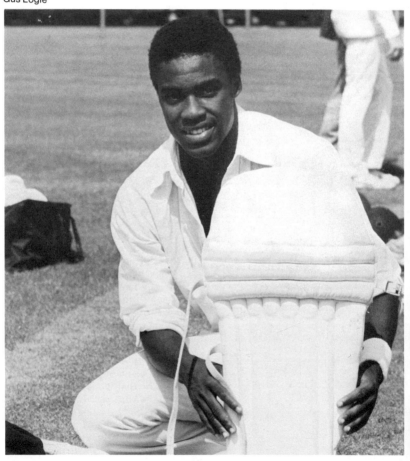

Ranjan Madugalle

Ranjan Madugalle
Born: April 22, 1959, Kandy, Ceylon.
Height: 5ft 7in.   *Weight:* 10st 4lb.
Right-handed batsman.
Teams: Nondescripts and Sri Lanka.

Career Highlights
1982: Scored unbeaten 91 against
  Pakistan.

He was unlucky enough to run out of partners, when he looked sure to score his maiden Test century against Pakistan at Karachi, 1982, when he was 91 not out. Madugalle was an automatic choice for Sri Lanka after they gained entry to Test cricket in 1982.

He had also played League cricket in England.

105

Majid Khan

Majid Khan

Born: September 28, 1946, Jullundur,
   India.
Height: 5ft 10in.   *Weight:* 12st 0lb.
Right-handed batsman, medium-
   paced or off-spin bowler.
Teams: Lahore, PIA, Punjab,
   Glamorgan, Cambridge University,
   Queensland and Pakistan.

Career Highlights
1976: Hit a century before lunch on the
   first day of Test match against New
   Zealand at Auckland.
1982: Became the highest-scoring
   Pakistani in Tests when he overtook
   Hanif Mohammad's previous record
   of 3,915 runs.

Majid Khan's cricket pedigree was perfect. His father, Dr Jehangir Khan, was
a pre-War Cambridge Blue and Indian
Test cap. His elder brother, Asad,
played the first class game and was a
Blue at Oxford in the sixties. And two
cousins, Javed Burki and Imran Khan,
have also captained Pakistan.

While Majid first played Test cricket in 1964, it was not until eight years
later and another 19 innings that he
made his first century, 158 off Australia at Melbourne. Then he was batting No. 4, but he later moved up to
open and in this role he hit a spectacular 108 not out before lunch
against New Zealand in 1976. Only the
Australians, Victor Trumper, Charles
Macartney and Sir Donald Bradman
(all against England) can match that
achievement on the first day of a Test.

He is an elegant batsman whose hitting can nevertheless border on the
violent. He struck 13 sixes in an innings for the Pakistanis against
Glamorgan in 1967. The following
season he joined that county and in
1969 helped them win the Championship with 1,547 runs, later captain-

ing them before leaving after 10 years.
He went up to Cambridge from 1970
to 1972 and led them in successive
years, also securing their first win over
Oxford in 14 seasons. It was surprising
that he captained Pakistan only three
times, in the home series against
England in 1973.

Majid looked past his best on the
1982 tour to England, doing just
enough to creep past Hanif's record as
the leading Pakistani scorer of all time,
before this record was taken by Zaheer
and Javed the following winter.

Ashok Mankad

Born: October 12, 1944, Bombay,
   India.
Height: 5ft 9in.   *Weight:* 11st 9lb.
Right-handed batsman.
Teams: Bombay and India.

Career Highlights
1975-76: Captained Bombay to victory
   in the Ranji Trophy, India's most
   prestigious domestic competition.
1976-77: Averaged 206, totalling 827
   runs, in Trophy matches.
1981: Hit 265 in Ranji Trophy final
   against Delhi at Bombay.

Ashok is the eldest son of the late
Vinoo Mankad, the great Indian all-
rounder of the forties and fifties. Not in
the same class as his father, Ashok has
nevertheless been good enough to play
22 Tests for his country. He has not
managed a century, although early on
in his international career he made a
valuable 97 as an opener when India
scored a famous victory over Australia
at Bombay, 1969.

Ashok has surpassed his father in
one respect. He holds the all-time
record for the number of Ranji Trophy
runs in a career, his total standing at
6,619 in 1983, when he also scored his

22nd century (150 not out against Orissa at Bombay) to draw level with Vijay Hazare.

Mansoor Akhtar

Born: December 25, 1956, Karachi, Pakistan.
Height: 5ft 7in.   *Weight:* 10st 12lb.
Right-handed batsman, and medium-paced bowler.
Teams: Karachi, United Bank and Pakistan.

Career Highlights
1977: Scored 224 not out in a world record opening stand of 561 with Waheed Mirza for Karachi Whites *v* Quetta.

Mansoor and his partner assured themselves of a place in the record books, when they overtook the previous record for the first wicket of 555 set by Herbert Sutcliffe and Percy Holmes for Yorkshire against Essex at Leyton in 1932. Although the match was given first class status, the fact that the stand took only six and a half hours cast doubt about the quality of the opposition. A further statistical quirk: Mansoor and Waheed also opened the bowling in both innings.

Mansoor has shown signs, not least in England in 1982, that he could blossom at international level and he scored his first Test century (111) at Faisalabad against Australia that year.

Vic Marks

Born: June 25, 1955, Middle Chinnock, Somerset, England.
Height: 5ft 9in.   *Weight:* 11st 8lb.
Right-arm off-spin bowler and right-handed batsman.
Teams: Somerset, Oxford University and England.

Career Highlights
1975-78: An Oxford Blue and captain of the team in 1976-77.

Mansoor Akhtar

Vic Marks

1983: England's best bowler of the World Cup with 13 wickets at an average of 18.92. Man of the Match in the NatWest Trophy final at Lord's when his bowling secured Somerset's victory over Kent.

Marks is an off-spin bowler of great value in limited overs cricket, but embarked on England's winter tour of 1984 with a question mark against his ability in Tests. His total confusion when he failed to spot the googly of Pakistani bowler Abdul Qadir in the Leeds Test of 1982 prompted the remark *'Whatever Marks read at Oxford, it wasn't leg spin.'* In fact, it was Classics!

Rodney Marsh

Born: November 4, 1947, Armadale,
Western Australia, Australia.
Height: 5ft 8½in.   *Weight:* 13st 3lb.
Wicket-keeper, left-handed batsman.
Teams: Western Australia and
Australia.

Career Highlights
1975-76: Equalled record of 26 victims
in a series (all caught), against West
Indies.
1981: Overtook Knott to hold record
for number of dismissals in a Test
career.
1982: Only 'keeper to reach Test
double of 3,000 runs and 300
dismissals.

To most cricket followers, English
especially, Rodney Marsh is the
archetypal Australian. Aggressively
competitive, and spectacular when
standing back to the fast bowlers who
have provided him with most of his victims, he has played a leading role in
many of his country's successes since
he made his debut in 1970. Then,
against Ray Illingworth's Ashes-
winning England team, he was played
ahead of better 'keepers in order to
boost Australia's batting. His deficien-
cies earned him the nickname 'Iron
Gloves', but a decade later he could
look back on his early career with
enough humour to title his
autobiography *Gloves of Irony*.
Whatever his apparent manner on the
field, he has retained a sense of
sportsmanship with opponents, to the
extent that he is always among the first
to share a beer with them after a hard
day's play.

His elder brother, Graham, is a
world class golfer, although both
played cricket for their state at
schoolboy level. When Rodney made
his debut as a senior it was as a batsman, scoring 104 against the West
Indies in 1968. He became the first
Australia wicket-keeper to score a century in a Test, with 132 against New
Zealand at Adelaide, 1974.

Statistically, the most successful
Test wicket-keeper of all time, he had
355 dismissals from 95 Tests after
1983-84 series against Pakistan.

It was fitting that his 264th Test
victim, which took him past Alan
Knott's then record total, should be a
catch off Dennis Lillee against
England at Leeds, 1981. Their careers
have run parallel with state and country, having both made their international debuts in the same series 11
years previously. They have also
shared controversy, none less than
when they both struck successful bets
at 500-1 for Australia to lose that Test.
But nobody could ever accuse Rodney
Marsh of not trying ... whatever the
occasion and whatever the stakes.

Malcolm Marshall

Born: April 18, 1958, St Michael,
Barbados.
Height: 5ft 11in.   *Weight:* 12st 0lb.
Right-arm fast bowler, right-handed
batsman.
Teams: Barbados, Hampshire, and
West Indies.

Career Highlights
1982: His 134 wickets in England is
the best by any bowler since the
reduction in the number of
Championship matches in 1969.

Malcolm Marshall's improvement during 1982 and 1983 elevated him from a
position as West Indies' fifth seamer to
the spearhead of their attack. He
generates most of his pace from a high
speed run, which makes it all the more
extraordinary that he is able to keep

going for long spells. He took 21 wickets in the 1983 home series against India in 1983, then was easily West Indies' most economical bowler in the World Cup, his 12 victims costing only 14 each. He completed another successful season with Hampshire, not only topping their bowling, but also hitting two centuries, to confirm his arrival as an all-rounder.

He went on West Indies return tour to India with a reputation to protect and immediately secured their crushing victory in the first Test at Kanpur. He whipped out the first four Indian batsmen in each innings.

Malcolm Marshall

Greg Matthews

Born: December 15, 1959, Newcastle,
New South Wales, Australia.
Height: 5ft 9in.   *Weight:* 11st 0lb.
Right-arm off-spin bowler, left-handed
batsman.
Teams: New South Wales and
Australia.

Career Highlights
1983: Scored 75 on Test debut for
Australia *v* Pakistan, Melbourne.

Greg Matthews made his mark in Sydney grade cricket with Western Sub-
urbs, the club which also produced
former Australian captain Bobby
Simpson. Matthews got into the New
South Wales state team which won the
Sheffield Shield in the 1982-83 season,
showing ability as a middle-order batsman with 343 runs in seven matches. A
year later he was filling the all-
rounder's berth in the Australian Test
team. He played the last two matches
of the 1983-84 series against Pakistan,
having earlier in the season hit 86 off
the tourists for New South Wales.

Everton Mattis

Born: April 11, 1957, Kingston,
Jamaica.
Height: 6ft 4in.   *Weight:* 13st 3lb.
Right-handed batsman, off-spin
bowler.
Teams: Jamaica and West Indies.

Career Highlights
1980: 132 for Jamaica *v* Guyana, at
Mobay.
1981: Took four for 42 for West Indies
against England, at Kingston.

Everton Mattis made all four of his
Test appearances against England
when they visited West Indies in 1981.
Although he was Jamaica's leading

scorer that season (579 runs in nine
matches) and again in 1982 (441 runs
in five matches) his country could
afford to ignore him. But Mattis said
he could not afford to turn down the
money when he joined the West
Indians in South Africa in 1983.

Rick McCosker

Born: December 11, 1946, Inverell,
New South Wales, Australia.
Height: 6ft 2in.   *Weight:* 12st 9lb.
Right-handed batsman.
Teams: New South Wales and
Australia.

Career Highlights
1974: Four centuries in successive
innings for New South Wales.
1982-83: Captained his State to their
first Sheffield Shield championship
for 17 years.

Rick McCosker had a meteoric rise in
the mid-seventies. He did not make his
first class debut until 1973, when he
got into the New South Wales team as
a number six. The following year he
had a phenomenal run and, at the age
of 28, was called up to open Australia's
batting in the fourth Test against
England. He took the same neat, mostly unexciting, style into the Test
arena, where he made four centuries
before joining Kerry Packer's World
Series Cricket.

Post-Packer, he lost his Test place,
but has continued to serve New South
Wales well. In their Sheffield Shield
triumph of 1982-83, McCosker played
a captain's part with 1,153 runs, three
centuries and an average of 54.90.

Duleep Mendis

Born: August 25, 1952, Moratuwa,
Ceylon.

Height: 5ft 5in.   *Weight:* 11st 11lb.
Right-handed batsman, occasional
  wicket-keeper.
Teams: Sinhalese and Sri Lanka.

Career Highlights
1982: The first Sri Lankan to hit two
  centuries in a Test match, *v* India, at
  Madras.

Duleep Mendis is an experienced batsman, a strong leg-side player especially, who has taken part in three World
Cup tournaments and whose 64 earned
him the man of the match award in the
surprise win over India in 1979.

He joined two greats in Bradman
and Weekes when he scored 105 in
both innings at Madras, in 1982, as the
only three players to score two centuries in a Test against India. Duleep
took over the Sri Lanka captaincy in
1983.

Geoff Miller

Born: September 8, 1952,
  Chesterfield, Derbyshire, England.
Height: 6ft 2in.   *Weight:* 11st 6lb.
Right-arm off-spin bowler and right-
  handed batsman.
Teams: Derbyshire and England.

Geoff Miller

Career Highlights

1978-79: Member of England's Ashes
winning team, and topped those
averages with 23 wickets at an
average of 15.04 as well as scoring
234 runs. Returned best figures of
five for 44 at Sydney.

1981: Helped Derbyshire win the
NatWest Trophy.

1982: Took eight for 70 against
Leicestershire at Cleveland.

Geoff Miller, a stubborn defensive
batsman and an off-spin bowler, has
made 32 appearances for England
since 1976. He has never quite
managed to dominate with either bat
or ball, but has scored 1,171 runs and
taken 59 wickets. He captained his
country from 1979 to the middle of
1981.

Mohammad Nazir

Born: March 8, 1946, Rawalpindi,
Pakistan.
Height: 5ft 6in.   *Weight:* 11st 0lb.
Right-arm off-spin bowler.
Teams: Railways and Pakistan.

Career Highlights

1969: Began Test career by taking
seven for 99 against New Zealand at
Karachi.

After a promising start to his international career, Nazir made little
impression on England's batsmen
when they toured in 1972-73, and he
was ignored by the Pakistan selectors
until the 1980-81 series against West
Indies, when he was again among the
wickets and had a return of five for 44
at Faisalabad. He topped the Pakistan
national bowling averages in 1981-82
to earn further chances at Test level,
although he was omitted from the 1983
World Cup start.

He toured Australia in 1983-84,
after some success in the series against
India which preceded the trip. He is
sometimes referred to as Nazir Junior.

Mohsin Khan

Born: March 15, 1955, Karachi,
Pakistan.
Height: 5ft 1½in.   *Weight:* 12st 2lb.
Right-handed batsman.
Teams: Railways, Habib Bank and
Pakistan.

Mohsin Khan

Career Highlights

1978: Mohsin (220) and Ashad Pervez (220) set a second wicket record for a match in Pakistan by adding 426 for Habib Bank against the Income Tax Dept in the semi-final of the Patron's Trophy, at Lahore.

1982: Hit 200 at Lord's to set up Pakistan's first win over England for 28 years, going on to become the first Pakistani to complete 1,000 Test runs in a calendar year.

Another of the class batsmen in the Pakistani line-up. Mohsin made his first class debut as a teenager in the 1970-71 season, but at the start of his career often paid for over ambitious stroke-play. He was picked against England at Karachi in 1978, yet had to wait three years, when he scored 1,160 runs in a season with Habib Bank, for a regular place.

He was one of the stars of the 1982 tour to England, with 1,248 runs, including two double centuries. Against Australia at Karachi, in September 1982, Mohsin had the unusual experience of being given out 'handled the ball'.

Mudassar Nazar

Born: April 4, 1956, Lahore, Pakistan.
Height: 5ft 9in.   *Weight:* 11st 9lb.
Right-handed batsman and medium paced bowler.

Mudassar Nazar

Teams: Lahore, Punjab, Combined Universities, Habib Bank, PIA, United Bank and Pakistan.

Career Highlights
1982: Match-winning six for 32 gained Pakistan surprise victory over England at Lord's.
1982-83: Compiled 761 runs in six-match series *v* India, including third wicket stand at Hyderabad of 451 with Javad Miandad which equalled record partnership for all Tests. Mudassar's share was 231.

Mudassar is the son of Nazar Mohammad, who played for Pakistan in the 1950s before an arm injury forced his retirement. A cricketer of great enthusiasm, Mudassar now is unrecognisable from the player who, against England at Lahore in December 1977, scored the slowest Test century ever in 557 minutes, his final score of 114 occupying almost ten hours. His achievement as a bowler at Lord's in 1982 stunned the England team, though Mudassar assured everyone afterwards that he had modelled his action on Dennis Lillee's! Later that year, having formed a successful opening partnership with Mohsin Khan, Mudassar included three centuries in a Bradman-like sequence of heavy scoring against India and passed 2,000 runs in his 35th Test.

David Murray

Born: May 29, 1950, St Michael, Barbados.
Height: 5ft 6in.   *Weight:* 9st 11lb.
Wicket-keeper, right-handed batsman.
Teams: Barbados and West Indies.

Career Highlights
1978: Scored 206 not out for West Indians against East Zone, at Jamshedpur.
1979: Five catches in Test innings *v* India, at Delhi.

For many years the understudy with the West Indies squad to his famous namesake, Deryck Murray, David finally got his chance when the latter joined the Kerry Packer troupe in 1978.

But in 1983, having that winter lost his place to Jeff Dujon in the West Indies team, Murray opted to play with the unofficial team in South Africa. His decision caused something of an international furore, as he was living in Australia and it seemed that he would be denied re-entry to that country, even though his wife was Australian.

Chris Old

Born: December 22, 1948, Middlesbrough, Cleveland, England.
Height: 6ft 3in.   *Weight:* 14st 7lb.
Right-arm fast medium bowler, left-handed batsman.
Teams: Yorkshire, Warwickshire, Northern Transvaal and England.

Career Highlights
1977: Hit the third fastest century of all time in 37 minutes for Yorkshire against Warwickshire.
1978: Took four wickets in five balls against Pakistan at Birmingham on the way to best England return of seven for 50.
1983: Passed a career total of 1,000 wickets.

Chris Old is one of several fast medium bowlers suspended from playing for England following the unofficial tour to South Africa in 1982. His England career has frequently been interrupted by injuries, otherwise he might have

David Murray

enjoyed a greater return than his 143 wickets in 46 Tests.

'Chilly' as he is nicknamed (C. Old) first played for England in December 1972 against India at Calcutta, claiming six wickets in the match and going on to increase this to 15 in the four matches he played that series. A menacing left-handed batsman against spin, he has half a dozen first class centuries to his name, but has rarely come off in Tests.

He played for Yorkshire from 1966 until 1982, when he was relieved of the captaincy and moved to Warwickshire. He was suspended for three days in 1983 by the Test and County Cricket Board, because newspaper articles which appeared under his name criticised former colleagues at Yorkshire.

Old is an intelligent bowler, able to bowl a dangerous outswinger and deceptively vary his pace. His brother, Alan, is an England rugby union stand-off and, in February 1974, they shared the distinction of being on international duty on opposite sides of the world on the same day – Chris against West Indies at Port of Spain and Alan against Ireland at Twickenham.

Albert Padmore

Born: December 17, 1946, St. James, Barbados.
Height: 6ft 2in.   *Weight:* 13st 3lb.
Right-arm off-spin bowler.
Teams: Barbados and West Indies.

Career Highlights
1976: Took 59 wickets on West Indies tour of England, including six for 69 against Middlesex at Lord's.
1980 and 1982: Captained Barbados to Shell Shield success.

Albert Padmore looked in the early

seventies to be the natural successor to Lance Gibbs as the West Indies No. 1 off-spinner. But he played only two Tests before excluding himself from any further consideration by joining the rebel tour to South Africa in 1983.

He also played World Series Cricket and had figures of six for 81 in a 'super-Test' between West Indies and Australia at Port of Spain in 1979.

John Parker

Born: February 21, 1951, Dannevirke, New Zealand.
Height: 5ft 11in.   *Weight:* 11st 12lb.
Right-handed batsman and occasional leg-spin bowler.
Teams: Northern Districts, Worcestershire and New Zealand.

Career Highlights
1975: Hit best Test score of 121 *v* England at Auckland; scored two centuries in a match (117 and 102 not out) for Northern Districts *v* Central Districts.
1981-82: Averaged 103 to top New Zealand averages in domestic season.

John Parker was the youngest of three brothers to play first class cricket. He followed the Glenn Turner trail to Worcestershire, but, despite being capped in 1974, had only moderate success and parted company with them after the 1975 season, his fourth in England.

He captained his country once, against Pakistan at Karachi in 1976, in the same match in which one of his brothers, Murray, made his Test debut.

John hit 108 as an opener against Australia at Sydney in 1974, when rain robbed New Zealand of a good winning chance. He later moved down the order and made his best Test score (121 *v* England at Auckland, 1975)

Paul Parker

Born: January 15, 1956, Bulawayo,
Rhodesia.
Height: 5ft 10½in.   *Weight:* 12st 0lb.
Right-handed batsman.
Teams: Sussex, Natal and England.

Career Highlights
1976: Scored 215 as a freshman for
Cambridge University *v* Essex,
obtaining a blue in three successive
years.

1978: Unbeaten 62 helped Sussex win
Gillette Cup final against Somerset.
1980-81: Played in Natal side which
won Currie Cup and followed with
best season for Sussex (1,412 runs).

A gifted sportsman (only injury prevented him winning a rugby union blue
in 1977) and a brilliant cover fielder,
he is another of the younger English
batsmen to have faltered after a bright
start to his career. He regressed after

Paul Parker

failing in his one game for England against Australia, 1981. Vice-captain of Sussex, he was even dropped by his county in 1983 when a miserable season for him yielded only 512 runs.

His father, John, played for Essex 2nds and was sports editor of Independent Television News.

Derick Parry

Born: December 22, 1954, Nevis, Leeward Isles.
Height: 5ft 11½in.   *Weight:* 12st 0lb.
Right-arm off-spin bowler.
Teams: Leeward Isles and West Indies.

Career Highlights
1978: Took five for 15 and scored 65 for West Indies *v* Australia, Port of Spain.
1980: Shell Shield record of 15 wickets in a match, including nine for 76 in the second innings, for Combined Islands *v* Jamaica at Kingston.

Derick Parry has had the misfortune to be playing as an off-spinner when his country has relied almost entirely on a pace attack for its success. He made his Test debut in 1978 against Australia at Port of Spain and recorded an ignominious double, out first ball and sending down a wide first ball when he bowled. Later in the series, at the same venue, he helped West Indies to a victory with match figures of 87 runs and six wickets.

He took 40 wickets on the 1980 tour to England yet was unable to get into the Tests and he had made only 12 appearances for his country, picking up 23 wickets, when he joined the West Indian rebels in South Africa in 1983. Derick has played Minor Counties cricket for Cambridgeshire since 1981 and has proved a useful all-rounder for them.

Len Pascoe

Born: February 13, 1950, Bridgetown, Western Australia, Australia.
Height: 6ft 1½in.   *Weight:* 14st 3lb.
Right-arm fast bowler.
Teams: New South Wales and Australia.

Career Highlights
1980: Wrecked England's first innings in Centenary Test at Lord's with five for 59, all his wickets coming in a 32-ball spell.
1982: Took eight for 41 for New South Wales against Tasmania at Hobart.

Of Croatian descent, Pascoe was born Len Durtanovich, but had changed his name by the time he made his first class debut in 1974-75. Genuinely quick during the late seventies, Pascoe took five wickets on his Test debut against England in 1977 at Lord's, when he partnered Jeff Thomson with the new ball in the absence of Dennis Lillee. He claimed 41 victims on the tour, but missed Australia's next full trip to England four years later because of injury.

Sandeep Patil

Born: August 8, 1956, Bombay, India.
Height: 6ft 1in.   *Weight:* 13st 2lb.
Right-handed batsman and right-arm medium-paced bowler.
Teams: Bombay and India.

Career Highlights
1981: Hit 174 against Australia at Adelaide, including a six and 22 fours, off only 240 balls.

The Indian with the playboy image has been trying to build a dual career as a cricketer and a film star. He can be a brilliant stroke-maker, as Australia found out in 1981.

Len Pascoe

He defied England at Manchester, 1982, with an unbeaten 129 including six 4s in an over off Bob Willis and showed his liking for the ground in the World Cup a year later. His unbeaten 51 contributed greatly to India's semi-final defeat of England.

He has played club cricket in London for Edmonton.

Sandeep Patil

Gerald Peckover

Born: June 2, 1955, Salisbury,
Rhodesia.
Height: 5ft 9in.   *Weight:* 10st 11lb.
Wicket-keeper, right-handed batsman.
Teams: Rhodesia and Zimbabwe.

Career Highlights
1977: Made 93 in debut match for
Rhodesia *v* Eastern Province at
Bulawayo.

A stylish batsman who can open the
innings, although his opportunities
were limited in the 1983 World Cup. A
brilliantly fast outfielder when he is not
keeping wicket, he is also a top class
hockey player.

Norbert Phillip

Born: June 12, 1949, Bioche,
Dominica.
Height: 6ft 0in.   *Weight:* 12st 4lb.
Right-arm fast bowler, right-handed
batsman.
Teams: Windward Islands, Essex and
West Indies.

Career Highlights
1978: Scored 134 against
Gloucestershire, at Gloucester.
1981: Took seven for 33 for Windward
Islands *v* Leeward Islands at Roseau.
1983: Hat trick for Essex *v* Northants
at Wellingborough.

Norbert Phillip played nine Tests for
West Indies, when they were forced to
widen their scope in the late seventies
because of defections to Kerry Packer's World Series Cricket.

He is a genuine all-rounder who has
contributed to Essex's modern success
in the English game. He helped them
win their first championship with 70
wickets in 1979, while his devastating
form spurred them to a repeat of that

success four years later. He caused a
sensation at Chelmsford in May by
bowling out Surrey for only 14, with
figures of six for four. He claimed six
victims in an innings four times that
season.

A typically West Indian batsman,
he scored 70 and 90 not out, as well as
getting 10 wickets, for Combined
Islands against Guyana, at
Georgetown, 1978 – but still finished
on the losing side!

Wayne Phillips

Born: March 1, 1958, Adelaide, South
Australia, Australia.
Height: 5ft 11in.   *Weight:* 11st 7lb.
Left-handed batsman and occasional
wicket-keeper.
Teams: South Australia and Australia.

Career Highlights
1983: Scored 159 on his Test debut, *v*
Pakistan, at Perth.

The left-handed opener Wayne
Phillips is the 14th Australian to have
scored a century in his first Test, and
his score of 159 is the fourth highest by
an Australian debutant, behind
Charles Bannerman's 165 in 1877,
Archie Jackson's 164 in 1929, and
Kepler Wessels's 162 in 1982.

Wayne spent the 1981 season in
England on an Esso scholarship,
establishing himself in the South Australia side on his return. In January
1982 at Adelaide, he made 260 in
seven and a half hours against Queensland, an innings all the more remarkable because most of it was played
while he was suffering from a stomach
upset. That season he helped South
Australia win the Sheffield Shield. He
was consistent, if less spectacular, the
following year and had to wait until
1983-84, when he began with a double

hundred off Tasmania and 75 against the touring Pakistanis, for his Test chance.

Pat Pocock

Born: September 24, 1946, Bangor, Gwynedd, Wales.
Height: 6ft 1½in.   *Weight:* 13st 0lb.
Right-arm off-spin bowler, right-handed batsman.
Teams: Surrey, Northern Transvaal and England.

Career Highlights
1968: Best bowling for England was six for 79 against Australia at Manchester. Earlier that year proved his worth as a dogged tail-end batsman by adding 109 with Tony Lock for the ninth wicket against West Indies at Georgetown – a record for that wicket between the two countries.
1972: Took seven wickets in 11 deliveries (including four in four balls).

Pat Pocock seems to have been classified as 'luxury item – for export only' by England's selectors. He made his Test debut as a 21-year-old against the West Indies at Bridgetown in 1968, but was chosen only 16 more times and given only three caps in England. Even after his best Test return he was dropped! He has been on five England tours and his Test haul stands at 47 wickets.

His most successful season for Surrey was in 1967, when he claimed 112 victims. Throughout most of his career, the Oval wicket has proved far less receptive to his spin bowling than it did in the heyday of Laker and Lock in the fifties. His best return was nine for 57 against Glamorgan at Cardiff in 1979.

He played the 1971-72 overseas season in South Africa, helping Northern Transvaal win the Currie Cup B Section.

Graeme Pollock

Born: February 27, 1944, Durban, South Africa.
Height: 6ft 2½in.   *Weight:* 13st. 8lb.
Left-handed batsman and occasional leg-spin bowler.
Teams: Eastern Province, Transvaal and South Africa.

Career Highlights
1960: Youngest player to score century in South African first class cricket – 16 years and 335 days when he made 102 for Eastern Province *v* Transvaal B in Johannesburg.
1963: Youngest player to hit double century in South African first class cricket – 19 years and 20 days when he made 209 not out for an Eastern Province Invitation XI against the International Wanderers at Port Elizabeth.
1970: His 274 off Australia at Durban in February is highest Test score by a South African.

Graeme Pollock was recognised as a batting genius, when politics cut short his Test career after 23 matches and 2,256 runs, with seven centuries. At that time his only rival as the world's best left-hander was Gary Sobers.

Pollock came from a cricketing family. His father, a native of Scotland, kept wicket for Orange Free State and his brother Peter, a fast bowler, played 28 Tests, also with great success.

Graeme could have accepted lucrative contracts to play in England or Australia but, unlike other South African stars, he was not lured. He remained a formidable batsman even

Graeme Pollock

in his late thirties, scoring 100 in the first international against the rebel West Indian XI at Capetown in 1983.

His 175, in his fourth Test match, at Adelaide in 1964 drew praise, even from Sir Donald Bradman, as a masterpiece. Pollock added 341 for the third wicket with Eddie Barlow and this remained a record stand for South Africa.

In England in 1965, he scored 125 off 145 balls at Trent Bridge, an especially notable innings in view of the prevailing seam bowling conditions.

His records in South Africa include the highest number of centuries in a career, standing at 35 in 1983, as well as the best aggregate for Eastern Province (984 runs in 1974-75) and for Transvaal (961 in 1978-79).

Derek Pringle

Born: September 18, 1958, Nairobi, Kenya.
Height: 6ft 4½in.   *Weight:* 14st 7lb.
Right-arm medium-paced bowler, right-handed batsman.
Teams: Cambridge University, Essex and England.

Career Highlights
1979-82: Top of the class at

Derek Pringle

Cambridge University, where he scored 1,929 runs, winning three Blues (but prevented by Test match duty from captaining them in the 1982 Varsity match).

1981-82: Highest score of 127 (twice) for the University *v* Worcestershire and *v* Glamorgan.

Derek Pringle, a giant all-rounder, but with rather ungainly movement on the cricket field, was given his England chance after some tremendous performances for Cambridge. However, he hardly justified the selectors' faith, which was such that they even sent him on the 1982-83 tour to Australia and New Zealand. Pringle's top score in 11 innings was 47 not out and his fast-medium seam bowling claimed only 11 wickets in seven Tests.

However, with Essex in 1983 he showed signs of adjusting to a higher level and his international opportunity may come again.

Mike Procter

Born: September 15, 1946, Durban, South Africa.
Height: 5ft 10½in.   *Weight:* 13st 0lb.
Right-handed batsman and fast or off-spin bowler.
Teams: Gloucestershire, Natal, Western Province, Rhodesia and South Africa.

Career Highlights
1969-70: Took 26 wickets in four-match Test series against Australia, including six for 73 at Port Elizabeth.
1970-71: Scored centuries in six successive matches for Rhodesia, so equalling first class record shared by C. B. Fry and Sir Donald Bradman.
1971: Hit 1,786 runs in English season with Gloucestershire. Registered highest score of 254 for Rhodesia *v* Western Province.
1972: Took nine for 71 for Rhodesia against Transvaal at Bulawayo.
1977: Took 109 wickets for Gloucestershire.
1980: Scored 108 and took 14 for 76 for Gloucs *v* Worcs at Cheltenham.

Mike Procter and Barry Richards, two of the world's greatest cricketers, were born within 14 months of each other in

Mike Procter

the same South African city, Durban. Both first displayed their talents in England on the South African schools tour of 1963, when Richards was captain and Procter his deputy. Both played for Gloucestershire 2nds in 1965 but decided not to qualify for county selection. They returned three years later, when overseas stars were allowed special registration, Procter to Gloucestershire and Richards to Hampshire.

Procter was to be a major influence with the West Country county for the next 13 years, both as an all-rounder and then as an inspirational captain. While Richards was unique in the extraordinary amount of time he had to play his shots, Procter, while never crude, used his exceptional eye and great athleticism to bludgeon the ball

off the bat – or to propel it with an unorthodox 'windmill' bowling action at the stumps. He possessed a deadly in-swinger and four times in first class cricket he achieved the hat trick, as well as in the Benson and Hedges Cup semi-final against Hampshire at Southampton in 1977, when he went on to lead Gloucestershire to victory in the final at Lord's against Kent. His batting (94) had given them success over Sussex in the Gillette final four years earlier.

Given the opportunities that Sobers and Botham have had in the international arena, Procter might have run them close for the title of cricket's finest all-rounder. A persistent knee injury forced him to leave Gloucestershire in 1981, but he continued to play in the South African season.

Andrew Pycroft

Born: June 6, 1956, Salisbury,
  Rhodesia.
Height: 5ft 10½in.   *Weight:* 11st 13lb.
Right-handed batsman.
Teams: South African Universities,
  Western Province B, Rhodesia and
  Zimbabwe.

Career Highlights
1982: Scored 133 for Zimbabwe *v*
  Pakistan International Airlines at
  Harare.

Pycroft, who plays his cricket with the
Harare Sports Club, has been Zimbabwe's most consistent batsman over
recent seasons, with centuries against
Leicestershire, PIA and Sri Lanka
touring sides. However, he had a disappointing 1983 World Cup, but was
back in the groove during the 1983-84
season with 469 runs in eight innings
against the Young West Indies.

Qasim Omar

Born: September 2, 1957, Kenya.
Height: 5ft 6in.   *Weight:* 9st 11lb.
Right-handed batsman.
Teams: Muslim Commercial Bank and
  Pakistan.

Career Highlights
1982: Became the sixth Pakistani to
  score a double century and a century
  in the same match with 210 not out
  and 110 for MCB against Lahore.
1983: Maiden Test century, 113 *v*
  Australia in Adelaide.

The first East African-born player to
represent Pakistan, Qasim Omar made
a tremendous impression in the 1982-
83 Pakistan season with his exciting
strokeplay. He passed 1,000 runs
before the turn of the year and
altogether hit five centuries and

averaged over 100 in the Quaid-e-
Azam Trophy.

   He made his Test debut against
India in September 1983 and went on
the succeeding tour to Australia. There
he hit his maiden Test century of 113,
thanks to a sporting gesture by Australia's Kepler Wessels. Omar was
given out caught at 52, but Wessels
indicated that the ball had not carried.

Carl Rackemann

Born: June 3, 1960, Wondai,
  Queensland, Australia.
Height: 6ft 4in.   *Weight:* 14st 7lb.
Right-arm fast bowler.
Teams: Queensland and Australia.

Career Highlights
1982: Took seven for 49 for
  Queensland against South Australia,
  at Brisbane.
1983: Took 11 wickets in his second

Carl Rackemann

Test *v* Pakistan at Perth.

Big Carl Rackemann had been earmarked for the Australian Test team from the season of his debut, 1979-80, when he took 17 wickets as a 19-year-old rookie for Queensland. He was sent on an Esso Scholarship to England in 1981, playing for Surrey in the Second XI championship.

He won his first Test chance against England on his home ground of Brisbane in November 1982, but missed the next match through injury and that was his only appearance of the series, although he topped the Australian national bowling averages. He made much more of an impact a year later against the Pakistanis, with five for 32 and six for 86 at Perth to bowl Australia to an innings victory.

Clive Radley

Born: May 13, 1944, Hertford, Hertfordshire, England.
Height: 5ft 10in. *Weight:* 12st 0lb.
Right-handed batsman.
Teams: Middlesex and England.

Career Highlights
1965: Shares Middlesex sixth wicket record of 227 with Fred Titmus, set against South Africa at Lord's.
1978: Scored 158 *v* New Zealand in second Test appearance, after joining England's winter tour as replacement for injured Mike Brearley.
1980: Best season (1,491 runs).

Though not a stylish batsman, the improvising Clive Radley applied himself with good effect to the England cause. He played eight Tests in 1978, averaging 48.10 and scoring two centuries, before his limitations were exposed by quick bowlers on Australian wickets the following winter.

Clive Radley

Arjuna Ranatunge

Born: December 1, 1963, Colombo,
  Ceylon.
Height: 5ft 8in.   *Weight:* 11st 5lb.
Left-handed batsman.
Teams: Sinhalese and Sri Lanka.

Career Highlights
1982: Scored half century against
  England.
1983: Scored 90 versus Australia.

Ranatunge looked full of promise when
he played in Sri Lanka's first Test
match against England as an 18-year-
old batsman and hit a half-century in
the first innings. He has yet to
dominate at Test level, although he
had some success against the touring
Australians in 1983, making 90 in the
Test match at Kandy and hitting the
winning six in his unbeaten 55 which
clinched a one-day international at
Colombo.

Arjuna Ranatunge

Derek Randall

Born: February 24, 1951, Retford,
  Nottinghamshire, England.
Height: 5ft 8½in.   *Weight:* 11st 0lb.
Right-handed batsman.
Teams: Nottinghamshire and England.

Career Highlights
1977: Brilliant 174 in Centenary Test
  against Australia at Melbourne.
1979: Scored two centuries in a match
  (209 and 146), against Middlesex at
  Trent Bridge for Notts.
1981: Randall's 1,093 runs (average
  45.54) contributed to the county's
  first Championship for 52 years.
1983: Passed 2,000 Test runs during
  that year's series against New
  Zealand.

The number of runs Derek Randall has
scored for England tell only part of the
story; he has probably saved half as
many again with his brilliance in the
covers. There is no more popular
player in English cricket than 'Arkle' (a
tribute to his fitness), at least with his
dressing room colleagues and
spectators.

  The selectors have not always been
as tolerant of Randall's eccentricities
at the crease, although he is Notts'
most capped player, with 40 caps to
the end of 1983. When they have wanted to meddle with the middle order,
Randall has often been the sacrifice.
When they have wanted to experiment,
they have made him opener, a role he
dislikes. Randall has rarely com-
plained. In any other profession he
would have had a case for unfair dis-
missal when after topping England's
averages in Australia during 1982-83,
he found himself surplus to require-
ments for the following summer's
World Cup matches.

  His most memorable performances
have been in Australia: the brilliant

Derek Randall

174 at Melbourne in 1977 almost won the match for England after they had been set a target of 463. At Sydney two years later a determined 150, after England trailed by 142 on first innings, set up an improbable victory.

His wife, Liz, tells a tale of Randall at fielding practice: *'When we were first married, Derek used to throw the tea-cups behind his back and catch them. That was one way he got out of doing the dishes.'*

Ravi Ratnayeke

New Zealand and was a regular member of his country's World Cup team in 1983.

Ravi Ratnayeke

Born: May 2, 1960, Ceylon.
Height: 6ft 3in.   *Weight:* 13st 12lb.
Right-arm medium fast bowler, left-handed batsman.
Teams: Nondescripts and Sri Lanka.

Career Highlights
1982: Toured Pakistan.

He came into the Sri Lanka team during their 1982 three-Test tour of Pakistan, and shared the new ball with Asantha de Mel. He played five consecutive Tests, but his comparative experience was ignored for Sri Lanka's 1983 World Cup campaign.

Peter Rawson

Born: May 25, 1959, Salisbury, Rhodesia.
Height: 6ft 3in.   *Weight:* 14st 4lb.
Right-arm fast medium bowler and right-handed batsman.
Teams: Zimbabwe.

Career Highlights
1983: Took seven for 55 and 13 wickets in the same match for Zimbabwe against the Young Australians at Harare.

Rawson, who made his debut for Zimbabwe in 1982 against Worcestershire, went on to claim 50 wickets in his first eight first class matches. An improving batsman, he switched clubs in 1983-84 from Harare Sports to Alexandra, where he will have more opportunities to improve this side of his game. He was once captain of his country's hockey team.

Rumesh Ratnayake

Born: January 2, 1964, Colombo, Ceylon.
Height: 6ft 0in.   *Weight:* 12st 0lb.
Right-arm medium-fast bowler.
Teams: Sri Lanka.

Career Highlights
1983: Took 4 for 81 against New Zealand.

Rumesh was whisked into the Sri Lanka team while still a schoolboy and made his Test debut against New Zealand in 1983, just months after playing his first first class match. He put in a good performance to claim four for 81 in his second Test against

John Reid

Born: March 3, 1956, Auckland, New
Zealand.
Height: 5ft 11in.   *Weight:* 12st 10lb.
Left-handed batsman.
Teams: Auckland and New Zealand.

Career Highlights
1981: Scored unbeaten 123 in his third
Test match, *v* India at Christchurch.
Made 173 for Auckland against
Northern Districts and topped New
Zealand averages with 817 runs at
58.35.

This player is no relation to the former
New Zealand captain of the same
name. John is a schoolmaster, who
captained Auckland to victory in the
final of the 1983 Shell Cup.

Barry Richards

Born: July 21, 1945, Durban, South
Africa.
Height: 5ft 11in.   *Weight:* 12st 7lb.
Right-handed batsman and occasional
off-spin bowler.
Teams: Gloucestershire, Hampshire,
South Australia, Natal and South
Africa.

Career Highlights
1970: Scored 356 (325 of them in a
day) for South Australia *v* Western
Australia at Perth in November.
1973-74: Set record for highest
aggregate of runs, 1,285 by a South
African in a home season.

But for the politics which restricted
him to just four Test matches, Barry

Barry Richards

Viv Richards

Richards could become recognised as the greatest opening batsman in the game's history. His deeds in three countries, and especially the punishing manner in which he scored his runs, put him on a different plane from his contemporaries.

He thrashed all county bowlers in English cricket for a 10 year period from 1968, when he announced himself with Hampshire by scoring 2,395 runs. He left abruptly in 1978, declaring himself, to the dismay of his many admirers who always believed he epitomised the joy of the game, to be bored by the ease of his regular run getting. During his spell at Hampshire, it was ironic that the master from the land of apartheid should form such a feared opening partnership with a black West Indian, Gordon Greenidge.

Richards knew the value of his talent and was always on the look-out for a fresh challenge. He stormed Australia in 1970-71, having the previous season in South Africa played a major role in the 4-0 whitewashing of the Aussies Test team. He accepted a contract with South Australia, scored 1,538 runs at an average of 109.86 and helped his adopted State regain the Sheffield Shield.

Back with Natal in 1973-74, he set a record for a South African in a home season of 1,285 runs. Another best for a South African season, his six centuries in 1969-70, was later equalled by Mike Procter and Peter Kirsten.

Viv Richards

Born: March 7, 1952, St Johns
Antigua.
Height: 5ft 11in.   *Weight:* 13st 8lb.
Right-handed batsman and off-spin bowler.
Teams: Leeward Islands, Somerset, Queensland and West Indies.

Career Highlights
1976: Set Test record for most runs in a calendar year with 1,710, including best score for West Indies of 291 against England at the Oval.
1977: Scored 2,161 runs for Somerset.
1979: Matchwinner for his country in World Cup Final at Lord's with 138 against England.

Viv Richards is widely regarded as the world's finest batsman. He was at his peak from the mid to late seventies, before his form was slightly affected by a combination of eye trouble and staleness. However, whether he is playing from the textbook or with audacious improvisation, he is a batsman who brings joy to all spectators and despair to most bowlers.

He has probably done as much for Antiguan tourism as he has for West Indies cricket. Before the emergence of Richards and Andy Roberts, few people outside of the Foreign Office had heard of the Caribbean island.

Viv's father was a fast bowler and his two elder brothers also played cricket. Viv's entry to the first class game was delayed until he was 20 because of a two-year ban. He was given out caught, but indicated on his way to the pavilion that he had not hit the ball. The crowd were so incensed that they successfully demanded his reinstatement on threat of a riot!

He made his first trip to England in 1973 with Andy Roberts, both of them funded by a public subscription to be coached at the Alf Gover School in South London. By 1974 they were signed up for Somerset and Hampshire respectively. That winter Richards was given a batting place in preference to the great Rohan Kanhai on the West Indies tour of India and Pakistan.

His Test debut coincided with that of Gordon Greenidge and with Clive

Richie Richardson

Lloyd's first match as captain. Richards atoned for a first game failure by scoring an unbeaten 192 against India in the next. He batted five hours, hitting six 6s and twenty 4s.

Smokin' Viv had arrived. He was used as a makeshift opener, in which role he had a century and two 50s, on the West Indies tour of Australia which preceded the visit to England in 1976. Then he was back to number three, and in only four Tests he totalled 829 runs, the fourth highest ever for a series and the best by a West Indian cricketer.

He missed the Lord's Test because of illness, but has held the stage spectacularly at cricket's headquarters since, with three man of the match performances. His 138 in the 1979 World Cup final was perfectly paced; his 145 in the 1980 Test included 25 4s and one 6; and his unbeaten 132 in the 1981 Benson and Hedges final for Somerset was made out of 197 for three. His party piece has been to cart the wide ball outside off-stump over mid-wicket, into the Tavern Bar.

With more than 50 Tests behind him he has well over 4,000 runs and an average of nearly 60, which only Graeme Pollock of modern players can match. He has been second-in-command to West Indies' captain Clive Lloyd since 1981.

He is a gentle, but effective, off-spin bowler who fills in particularly well in one-day matches. He performed the hat trick against Essex in a 1982 Sunday League match.

Richie Richardson

Born: January 12, 1962, Antigua.
Height: 5ft 11in.　*Weight:* 11st 13lb.
Right-handed batsman.
Teams: Leeward Islands and West Indies.

Career Highlights
1983: Scored his maiden century (102) in his fifth first class innings for Leeward Islands against Barbados at Bridgetown in January and followed up in February with 156 off Jamaica at Plymouth, Montserrat.

Richardson became the latest Antiguan to make the Test scene, when he was picked at the age of 21 to play for West Indies against India, at Bombay in November 1983, having earlier that year come to prominence in the Shell Shield.

Greg Ritchie

Born: January 23, 1960, Stanthorpe, Queensland, Australia.
Height: 5ft 10in.   *Weight:* 13st 0lb.
Right-handed batsman.
Teams: Queensland and Australia.

Career Highlights
1982: Scored a century in his third Test innings – 106 not out *v* Pakistan at Faisalabad.

Greg Ritchie announced himself as a batsman with talent, when he scored an unbeaten 140 for Queensland against Victoria at Geelong in 1981. The following season he cracked three more centuries and booked a place on Australia's tour of Pakistan, where he played in all three Tests. However, he came unstuck in the 1982-83 season and failed to make the Test team for the Ashes series against England. However, he was back on the run trail in October 1983 with a career-best 196 against the Pakistani tourists at Brisbane.

Andy Roberts

Born: January 29, 1951, Urlings Village, Antigua.
Height: 6ft 1in.   *Weight:* 13st 8lb.
Right-arm fast bowler.
Teams: Leeward Islands, Combined Islands, Hampshire, New South Wales, Leicestershire and West Indies.

Career Highlights
1974: Took 119 wickets for Hampshire

Andy Roberts

at cost of 13.62 each.

1976: Passed 100 Test wickets in two years 140 days, a record until surpassed by Ian Botham.

Andy Roberts, son of a fisherman and one of a family of 14, became the first Antiguan to play for West Indies when he faced England in 1974. He was dropped after one game, but later that year established himself as one of the fastest bowlers around, when he took 119 wickets in the English season with consistently hostile bowling.

In the winter of 1974-75, he was the difference between victory and defeat for West Indies, who won a close series in India 3-2, thanks to Roberts setting a record for the series of 32 wickets.

The following year he was the

spearhead of the West Indies attack against Australia and he returned his best Test figures of seven for 54 at Perth, to give his side an innings victory. But it was to be the only success of a disheartening series from the West Indies' point of view, although Roberts finished with 22 wickets. By now Roberts had been joined in the side by Michael Holding and he was upstaged by his new partner when it came to speed. Robert's sad eyes and lack of words projected a mean and moody image. But he is an intelligent cricketer who later in his career has made good use of his ability to swing the ball.

He left Hampshire in 1978 after signing for Kerry Packer's circus, but returned to the English game on a part-time basis with Leicestershire. He took 105 wickets for Littleborough in the Central Lancashire League in 1982 and that winter showed he was still capable of bowling at the highest level with 24 wickets against India.

However, after the 1983 World Cup, he was again burdened by injuries.

Brian Rose

Born: June 4, 1950, Dartford, Kent, England.
Height: 6ft 1½in.   *Weight:* 13st 7lb.
Left-handed batsman.
Teams: Somerset and England.

Career Highlights
1979: Captained Somerset to Gillette Cup and John Player Sunday League double – the county's first honours and followed this up by leading them to successive Benson and Hedges Cup triumphs in 1981 and 1982.
1980: Averaged 48.60 in Test series against West Indies.

Of his eight Tests, Brian Rose played

two as an opener and the rest at No. 3. An attacking batsman, he hit a particularly forceful 70 out of England's total of 150 against West Indies at Manchester in 1980.

In his best season (1,624 runs), he hit two centuries in a match (124 and 150 not out) against Worcestershire in 1980. His career seemed to suffer after an eye defect forced him to return early from England's 1981 tour to West Indies. And in 1983 he was restricted by a back injury to just seven matches.

Lawrence Rowe

Born: January 8, 1949, Kingston, Jamaica.
Height: 5ft 9in.   *Weight:* 11st 2lb.
Right-handed batsman.
Teams: Jamaica, Derbyshire and West Indies.

Career Highlights
1972: Holds distinction of scoring a double century and a century in his first Test – 214 and 100 not out for West Indies against New Zealand at Kingston, Jamaica.
1974: Hit 302 against England at Barbados.

Lawrence Rowe led one of the most provocative moves in cricket history in January 1983, when he captained a rebel West Indian team to South Africa. He and his colleagues were banned for life from West Indian cricket.

Rowe, in the early stages of his career, threatened to set new standards in run getting. A cultured batsman, happy to open or go in No. 3 or 4, he chose his debut Test to become only the third player (after Doug Walters of Australia and Indian Sunil Gavaskar) to score a century and a double cen-

Lawrence Rowe

Balwinder Sandhu

tury in the same Test. In the 1974 series against England, he totalled 616 runs, including his triple century at Barbados.

From then on, his career, both with West Indies and Derbyshire, seemed jinxed. His main trouble was with his eyes. But he also suffered from an allergy to grass – a nightmare for a cricketer.

Balwinder Sandhu

Born: January 3, 1956, Bombay, India.
Height: 6ft 1in.   *Weight:* 14st 3lb.
Right-arm medium-fast bowler, right-handed batsman.
Teams: Bombay and India.

Career Highlights
1983: Member of India's World Cup-winning team.

Sandhu, a heavily built opening bowler, hit 71 batting at number nine in his first Test against Pakistan at Hyderabad, 1983. He retained his place in the following series against West Indies, and for the World Cup later that year. He bats with a helmet on top of his turban.

Sarfraz Nawaz

Born: December 1, 1948, Lahore, Pakistan.
Height: 6ft 3in.   *Weight:* 14st 4lb.
Right-arm fast medium bowler.
Teams: Lahore, United Bank, Northamptonshire and Pakistan.

Career Highlights
1979: Took nine for 86 in bowling Pakistan to a 71 runs victory over Australia at Melbourne.
1982-83: Completed 150 Test wickets in home series against India.

Sarfraz Nawaz is one of international cricket's great characters. He has been in a long-running battle with Pakistani officials, but there has been no denying his worth as a new ball bowler both for his country and for Northants in the English game.

He has a loping, almost laboured, run to the wicket. But at his fittest, his pace is brisk and his movement of the ball deceptive to even the best batsmen.

He first joined Northants in 1969, being released after three seasons. The

Sarfraz Nawaz

county had second thoughts, however, when a much-improved Sarfraz toured England with the Pakistanis in 1974 and he rejoined them before he finally parted company after the 1982 season, by which time his injury problems were becoming more frequent. His best year for them was in 1975, when he captured 101 wickets.

Sarfraz, a banker by profession, was banned by the Pakistani board in October 1983 for six months for 'gross violation' of the board's code of conduct. He had repeatedly criticised the chairman of selectors, Nur Khan, a habit which had already cost him a fine of £500. Sarfraz had been omitted from the tour party to Australia. The official reason was that he was unfit, but Sarfraz claimed it was because he had refused to agree to a Pakistan 'plan' to play for a draw in the 1983 series against India. All three matches were, in fact, drawn.

Mike Selvey

Born: April 25, 1948, Chiswick,
  London, England.
Height: 6ft 2in.   *Weight:* 14st 0lb.
Right-arm medium-paced bowler.
Teams: Cambridge University, Surrey,
  Middlesex, Glamorgan, Orange Free
  State and England.

Career Highlights
1976: Took a wicket with his sixth ball
  in Test cricket *v* West Indies, at
  Manchester. After 20 balls had three
  for six and finished with four for 21.
  Claimed seven for 20 for Middlesex
  against Gloucestershire the same
  year.

One of the most consistent – and intelligent – medium-paced bowlers in English county cricket, Selvey had his hour of glory as a Test match perfor-

mer, too. He received a last minute call to open the bowling for England against the powerful West Indies team of 1976. Despite a successful match – his first innings victims included Fredericks, Richards and Kallicharran – he made only two other Test appearances.

A Cambridge Blue, he turned out first for Surrey, spent ten seasons with Middlesex, then took on the Glamorgan captaincy in 1983.

Yashpal Sharma

Born: August 11, 1954, Ludhiana,
  India.
Height: 5ft 8in.   *Weight:* 12st 2lb.
Right-handed batsman, occasional
  wicket-keeper.
Teams: Punjab and India.

Yashpal Sharma

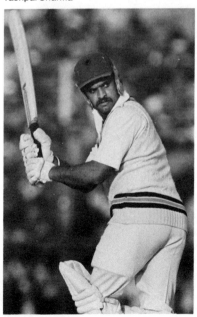

Ravi Shastri

Career Highlights
1982: Shared an Indian third wicket
   record stand of 316 with Gundappa
   Viswanath against England at
   Madras.

Yashpal has been an in and out member of the Indian team, since making
his debut against England in 1979. He
completed 1,500 Test runs during the
1983 series in West Indies. That summer he was a member of India's
triumphant World Cup team and in a
qualifying match played a significant
part in West Indies' first-ever defeat in
the competition, with an innings of 89.

Ravi Shastri

Born: May 27, 1962, Bombay, India.
Height: 6ft 2in.   *Weight:* 13st 0lb.
Slow left-arm bowler, right-handed
   batsman.
Teams: Bombay and India.

Career Highlights
1981: Dramatic first Test in New
   Zealand, when he flew from India to
   answer an injury crisis, arrived in
   Wellington on eve of match, and took
   six wickets.

Ravi Shastri, a former captain of
India's Under 19 team, is an all-
rounder of genuine talent. He batted
number 10 in his first Test, but two
years later scored his maiden century
for India, opening with Gavaskar
against Pakistan at Karachi. He added
a further 'ton' against West Indies in
the series that followed and, although
he missed out on the glory of India's
World Cup victory, he was back in the
side the following winter and took five
for 75 at Nagpur in the return series
against Pakistan. He and Gavaskar
added an Indian six wicket record *v*
West Indies of 170 at Madras in 1983.

John Shepherd

Born: November 9, 1943, St. Andrew,
    Barbados.
Height: 5ft 11in.   *Weight:* 12st 13lb.
Right-arm medium-paced bowler,
    right-handed batsman.
Teams: Barbados, Rhodesia, Kent,
    Gloucestershire and West Indies.

Career Highlights
1968: 170 for Kent *v* Northants at
    Folkestone.
1969: Five for 104 in 58 overs for West
    Indies *v* England at Lord's.
1977: Eight for 83 for Kent *v*
    Lancashire at Tunbridge Wells.
1983: 168 and seven for 50 for
    Gloucestershire *v* Warwickshire at
    Edgbaston.

John Shepherd is the longest-serving
overseas player in the English county
game. He made his first team debut for
Kent in 1966 and went on to help them
to three Championships (one shared),
three Benson and Hedges Cup vic-
tories and two Gillette Cup triumphs.

John Shepherd

Maninder Singh

He left them in 1983 for Gloucestershire and must have surprised even himself with some spectacular all-round performances, finishing the season with 67 wickets and 1,025 runs.

He played only five Tests for West Indies, including three in the short series in England in 1969. He distanced himself from his fellow countrymen in 1973 when he became the first black West Indian to tour in South Africa and later turned out for Rhodesia.

Sikander Bakht
Born: August 25, 1957, Karachi, Pakistan.
Height: 6ft 2in.   *Weight:* 11st 4lb.
Right-arm fast-medium bowler.
Teams: Sind, Karachi, United Bank and Pakistan.

Career Highlights
1979: Eight for 69 for Pakistan against India, Delhi.

Sikander was a regular member of the Pakistan team for six years after getting his chance at Test level in 1976. He is an energetic new ball bowler who curtailed England captain Mike Brearley's tour of Pakistan in 1977-78, when one of his deliveries broke his arm during a one-day match at Karachi.

Sikander lost his Pakistan place during the 1982-83 season, by which time he had taken 67 wickets in 26 Tests. He concentrated his efforts on the domestic scene and contributed towards United Bank's regaining of the Quaid-e-Azam Trophy with 30 wickets.

Maninder Singh
Born: June 13, 1965, Poona, India.
Height: 5ft 10in.   *Weight:* 9st 9lb.
Slow left-arm bowler.

Teams: Delhi and India.

Career Highlights
1981: Made his first class debut for Delhi against Punjab at 16 years old, taking 14 wickets.

Maninder Singh is seen as the new Bishen Bedi in Delhi ... and has the advantage of being coached by the former Indian spinner and captain.

Maninder was India's youngest cap, at 17 years 193 days, when he played his first Test against Pakistan at Karachi in December 1982. He showed signs the following year that he was beginning to come to terms with Test cricket with a return of four for 85 against the West Indies at Ahmedabad.

The slim-line youngster should certainly have the stamina for five-day cricket. In the 1982 Ranji Trophy final, he bowled 87.5 overs for Delhi as Karnataka ran up a score of 705.

Laxman Sivaramakrishnan

Born: December 31, 1965, India.
Height: 5ft 6in.   *Weight:* 9st 12lb.
Right-arm leg-spin bowler.
Teams: Tamil Nadu and India.

Career Highlights
1983: Youngest-ever Indian Test player.

Sivaramakrishnan became India's youngest-ever player (taking over from Maninder Singh) when he made his Test debut against West Indies at Antigua on April 28, 1983, aged 17 years and 118 days.

He had played his first Ranji Trophy match at 16, taking seven for 28 (nine wickets in the match) for Tamil Nadu against Delhi.

Peter Sleep

Born: May 4, 1957, Penola, South Australia.
Height: 5ft 11in.   *Weight:* 11st 10lb.
Right-arm leg-spin bowler, right-handed batsman.
Teams: South Australia and Australia.

Career Highlights
1979: Eight for 133 for South Australia *v* Victoria, at Melbourne.
1983: 144 for South Australia *v* Queensland at Brisbane.

Peter Sleep, a leg-spin bowler, is an anachronism as far as international cricket goes. He has made just four Test appearances since his debut at that level in 1979. However, he has continued to show his value as an all-rounder for South Australia and his 26 wickets, coupled with 438 runs, contributed to their winning of the Sheffield Shield in 1981-82.

Chris Smith

Born: October 15, 1958, Durban, South Africa.
Height: 5ft 11in.   *Weight:* 12st 12lb.
Right-handed batsman, occasional off-spin bowler.
Teams: Natal, Glamorgan, Hampshire and England.

Career Highlights
1983: Scored five centuries for Hampshire – including best-to-date 193 against Derbyshire.

Chris Smith drives a Porsche. His miles per hour are likely to be much faster than his runs per hour! He is an accumulative opening batsman rather than a dazzler. His dedication has drawn approval from the greatest practiser of them all, Geoff Boycott, though what Boycott said about yet *another*

Chris Smith

Ian Smith

foreigner playing for England isn't on record. Smith is the fifth South African (following d'Oliveira, two Greigs and Allan Lamb) to play for England in recent times. And if Smith's younger brother, Robin, is as good as his advance publicity, he will be the next when he qualifies in 1985.

Smith joined Hampshire in 1980 (having made his U.K. debut the previous season for Glamorgan v Sri Lanka) and topped 1,000 runs at his first attempt. His opportunities were then limited, as Hampshire used Gordon Greenidge and Malcolm Marshall as their overseas players, until Smith became 'English' in 1983.

He had an unhappy first Test for England at Lord's against New Zealand in 1983. He was out to his first ball – Richard Hadlee getting him lbw. He then had to endure a vociferous member telling him to get back to his wretched country.

He is a competitive squash player and a five-handicap golfer – his aunt, Jackie Mercer, was the leading South African ladies' golfer of her time.

Ian Smith

Born: February 28, 1957, Nelson, New Zealand.
Height: 5ft 8½in.   *Weight:* 12st 0lb.
Wicket-keeper, right-handed batsman.
Teams: Central Districts and New Zealand.

Career Highlights
1983: Regained his Test place for New Zealand's historic win over England at Leeds and took seven catches. Scored three centuries in the 1982-83 New Zealand season.

Ian Smith, an insurance representative, has vied with Warren Lees for the New Zealand wicket-keeper's role in recent years. He had been considered the weaker batsman, but his improved form in that role may now give him the edge over his rival. He certainly looked the cleaner wicket-keeper in England in 1983. He got into the New Zealand team on the 1980-81 tour to Australia, but a broken finger hampered his progress the following season.

Martin Snedden
Born: November 23, 1958, Auckland, New Zealand.

Martin Snedden

Height: 6ft 0in.   *Weight:* 12st 7lb.
Right-arm fast-medium bowler, left-handed batsman.
Teams: Auckland and New Zealand.

Career Highlights
1983: Seven for 49 against Canterbury at Auckland.
1984: Helped bowl out England for 220 in the first innings of their New Zealand tour with six for 70.

His batting is strong enough to rate him an all-rounder in New Zealand domestic cricket. But this lawyer, who is also a keen rugby player, always bats well down the order at international level. He suffered the indignity of being hit for 105 runs (a record for the competition) off his 12 overs by England in the 1983 World Cup.

Krishna Srikkanth

Born: December 21, 1959, Madras, India.
Height: 5ft 8in.   *Weight:* 10st 3lb.
Right-handed batsman.
Team: Tamil Nadu and India.

Career Highlights
1983: Member of India's World Cup winning team.

Srikkanth is an adventurous opening batsman, whose methods are likely to give most captains a heart attack, at least at Test level. However, he has been effective in one day matches and hit successive scores of 57, 95 and 92 against Sri Lanka in 1982. That winter he scored 83 and 110 for the Rest of India against Delhi.

He is a qualified electrical engineer.

Krishna Srikkanth

David Steele

Born: September 29, 1941, Stoke-on-Trent, Staffordshire, England.
Height: 5ft 11in.　*Weight:* 13st 7lb.
Right-handed batsman, slow left-arm bowler.
Teams: Northants, Derbyshire and England.

Career Highlights
1966: Best bowling is six for 29 against Lancashire at Northampton.
1971: Highest score 140 not out off Worcestershire.
1975: Best season for Northants when, 12 years after debut, he scored 1,756 runs (average 48.77).
1976: Scored only Test century, 106 for England *v* West Indies at Trent Bridge.
1978: For Northants against Derbyshire scored 130 and took six for 36 and six for 39.

David Steele became the most unlikely sporting hero of a nation in the summer of 1975. The bespectacled, white-haired, wise owl of the county circuit was summoned to the Test arena as England sought batsmen of substance who could face up to fast bowling. He countered the menace of Lillee and Thomson superbly, with a half century in his first innings and further scores of 45, 73, 92, 39 and 66. He didn't do badly next season, either, against the West Indies. Roberts and Holding held few terrors. But scores of 106, 6, 7, 64, 20, 15, 4, 0, 44 and 42 were to complete his brief but worthy Test career. Eight matches, 16 innings, an average of 42.06, a century and five 50s.

His style was never graceful but always unflinching. His short-term job was done and he returned to continue the work of a solid professional with Northants, Derbyshire (whom he captained for half a season in 1979) and

Northants again. His later years have seen him used more as a left-arm spin bowler. He returned to Northants in 1982 and in successive seasons gave them another 1,359 runs and 138 wickets.

With England, his careful habit around the bar earned him the cryptic nickname 'Crime' (does not pay!). At Northants they call him 'Stainless'. His younger brother, John, played for Leicestershire for 13 years.

Franklyn Stephenson

Born: April 8, 1959, Halli Village, Barbados.
Height: 6ft 3½in.　*Weight:* 13st 5lb.
Right-arm fast bowler. Right-handed batsman.
Teams: Barbados, Tasmania and Gloucestershire.

Career Highlights
1981: Six for 19 for Tasmania *v* Victoria, Melbourne.
1982: Scored 165 for Barbados *v* Leeward Isles, Basseterre.
1983: Took six for nine in one-day international, West Indies XI *v* South Africa at Durban.

Franklyn Stephenson, one-time hotel porter, threw up the chance of a Test career when he joined the West Indies rebels in South Africa in 1983 to spearhead their attack with Sylvester Clarke.

He was a great success for Tasmania in the 1981-82 season, finishing second in the Australian first class averages with 36 wickets. He then returned home to make his debut for Barbados and, going in as a nightwatchman, hit a cracking 165 (with four 6s and 20 4s). His next stop was England, where he fitted in seven matches for Gloucestershire, taking 25

Tahir Naqqash

wickets and topping the county's bowling averages, as well as helping Rawtenstall win the Lancashire League for the second year running with 519 runs and 99 wickets.

Graham Stevenson

Born: December 16, 1955, Hemsworth, Yorkshire, England.
Height: 6ft 0in.   *Weight:* 13st 0lb.
Right-arm fast medium bowler.
Teams: Yorkshire and England.

Career Highlights
1979-80: Went on tour with England to Australia and India (flown out as replacement) and following winter to West Indies.

Stevenson made his debut for Yorkshire in 1973, but was not capped until five years later – soon afterwards rocketing into the England reckoning. In 1980 he took 8 for 57 against Northants at Leeds. He enjoys a hefty swing as a late order batsman and in 1982, against Warwickshire at Birmingham, he hit 115 not out in a Yorkshire last wicket record stand of 149 with Geoff Boycott.

Tahir Naqqash

Born: July 6, 1959, Lahore, Pakistan.
Height: 5ft 10in.   *Weight:* 12st 0lb.
Right-arm fast medium bowler and right-handed batsman.
Teams: Punjab, Lahore, Muslim Commercial Bank and Pakistan.

Career Highlights
1982: Took five for 41 against England at Edgbaston, including Ian Botham first ball.

Tahir, son of a journalist, and a former off-spinner, has shown sufficient skill

Chris Tavare

as a batsman to develop as an all-rounder. He scored 57 in his first Test innings, against Sri Lanka at Karachi, 1982.

Chris Tavare

Born: October 27, 1954, Orpington, Kent, England.
Height: 6ft 1½in.   *Weight:* 12st 0lb.
Right-handed batsman.
Teams: Oxford University, Kent and England.

Career Highlights
1973: Made an early impression with 124 not out for England Schools *v* India Schools.
1981: Reached a Test personal best of 149 against India in Delhi. Hit 1,770 runs (average 55.63).
1983: With Graeme Fowler set opening stand record for England against New Zealand of 223 at the Oval in 1983. Led Kent to final of NatWest Trophy losing at Lord's to Somerset.

Chris Tavare made his Test debut in 1980. He has displayed skilful defence and great powers of concentration in establishing himself as England's anchorman in the role of opener. However, he much prefers the position of number three which he occupies for Kent, and from where he often shows off the range of strokes he leaves in cold storage while on international duty.

He gained a degree in zoology, while at Oxford from 1975-77, and has been called 'The Insect Man,' a not inappropriate label considering his long spells of inanimation at the crease! Against Australia at Manchester in 1981 he took 710 minutes to score 147 in two innings (69 and 78). And against India at Madras in 1982, he heeded captain Keith Fletcher's instruction's to bat as long as possible. He made his 35 last five and a half hours.

Bob Taylor MBE

Born: July 17, 1941, Stoke-on-Trent, Derbyshire, England.
Height: 5ft 9in.   *Weight:* 10st 0lb.
Wicket-keeper, right-handed batsman.
Teams: Derbyshire and England.

Bob Taylor

Career Highlights
1980: Set Test record of 10 dismissals in a match (all caught) *v* India in Bombay. In same game equalled the record of seven dismissals in an innings.
1981: Hit maiden first class century after 20 years in the game against Yorkshire at Sheffield.
1982-83: Overtook John Murray's world record of 1,527 victims in a career, during tour to Australia.

Bob Taylor played for Staffordshire in the Minor Counties when he was 15. Twenty six years later, with the banishment of Geoff Boycott, he was the oldest player still in Test cricket. The immaculate wicket-keeper, whose lively banter earned him the nickname 'Chat' in the England dressing room, built an international career at an age when most cricketers are living off the investment of their benefits. He was in his 43rd year when he embarked on England's 1984 tour of Pakistan and New Zealand. The selectors were so sure of his form and fitness that they did not send a regular second 'keeper with the party.

Until 1977 it seemed that, because of the brilliance of Alan Knott, Taylor would for ever be restricted to the one consolation cap he earned in New Zealand in 1971. Then Knott joined World Series Cricket, and Taylor, even at 36, was the automatic replacement. By 1983 he had become the first Derbyshire player to appear 50 times for England. He had claimed 162 victims.

It is ironic that in 1977 Taylor told Wisden: *'There are about 300 county cricketers and we can't all play for England.'*

Jeff Thomson

Born: August 16, 1950, Greenacre,
  Sydney, New South Wales, Australia.
Height: 6ft 1in.   Weight: 13st 4lb.
Right-arm fast bowler.
Teams: New South Wales, Queensland,
  Middlesex and Australia.

Career Highlights
1974-75: Took 33 wickets in five Tests
  against England, including six for 46
  at Brisbane.
1977: Completed 100 wickets in 22
  Tests during match against England
  at Lord's.

Jeff Thomson was regarded as a tearaway fast bowler who was unlikely to succeed at Test level . . . until he got to work on England during their 1974-75 tour of Australia. 'Tommo' became a terror with his speed and lift and, in partnership with Dennis Lillee, reduced many of England's batsmen to nervous wrecks. Thomson missed the sixth Test, after wrenching his shoulder while playing tennis on the rest day of the fifth, otherwise he could probably have broken the then record of 36 wickets in an Ashes series, set by Arthur Mailey in 1920-21.

Thomson had certainly made an enormous improvement since his Test debut against Pakistan two years earlier when he took none for 110. The fun-loving surf rider from Sydney was to have his injury problems and trouble with his run up in England, yet at his peak he has been one of the game's most destructive fast bowlers.

He and Dennis Lillee not only assured Australia of a 4-1 victory in that 1974-75 series against England, but the following season they tore into the powerful West Indies batting line-up, sharing 56 wickets and setting up a 5-1 win for Australia in an unofficial World Championship series.

In 1976, in a Test against Pakistan at Adelaide, Thomson was involved in a freak fielding accident, when he crashed into teammate Alan Turner and again damaged his shoulder, but he was still Australia's leading wicket-taker in the following year's series in England, with 22 victims.

He played a season with Kerry Packer's World Series Cricket and made eight appearances for Middlesex in 1981, when he was left off the Australian tour.

However, despite his gradual decline, he popped up again against England in the 1982 series and played

Jeff Thomson

his part in Australia's winning of the Ashes with 22 wickets at only 18.68 each. This took his Test aggregate to 197, the sixth highest of any Australian.

Roger Tolchard

Born: June 15, 1946, Torquay, Devon, England.
Height: 5ft 9in.　　*Weight:* 11st 6lb.
Wicket-keeper, right-handed batsman.
Teams: Leicestershire and England.

Career Highlights
1976-77: Played four Tests for England on tour of India, all as batsman.
1979: Shared county fifth wicket record stand of 223 with Nigel Briers against Somerset.

1981-83: Captained Leicestershire.

Tolchard was England's second choice wicket-keeper on three tours during the seventies, but was denied a chance behind the stumps by the form and fitness of, first, Alan Knott and then Bob Taylor. A valued member of Leicestershire's successful side of that period, he helped them to a County championship, two Benson and Hedges Cup triumphs and two Sunday League titles. He became the first wicket-keeper to complete the double of 1,000 runs and 100 victims in the Sunday League, achieving this in 1974 from 86 matches. Leicestershire, surprisingly, did not renew his contract for 1984 and he has taken a schools' coaching job instead.

Roger Tolchard

John Traicos

Peter Toohey

Born: April 20, 1954, Blayney, New South Wales, Australia.
Height: 5ft 10in.   *Weight:* 11st 0lb.
Right-handed batsman.
Teams: New South Wales and Australia.

Career Highlights
1978: Scored 122 and 97 in same Test match – Australia *v* West Indies, at Kingston, Jamaica.

Peter Toohey was one of the young batsmen Australia turned to during the defection of their stars to World Series Cricket in 1977 and he seemed to have seized his chance of a regular place by scoring 705 runs in his first eight Tests. However, he came unstuck against Mike Brearley's England team in 1978-79, his isolated success being 81 not out in the Perth Test match, although that season he continued in good form for his state, hitting a career-best 158 in four and three quarter hours against Western Australia in Sydney.

A food technologist, Toohey has remained a reliable middle-order batsman for New South Wales, helping win the Sheffield Shield in 1982-83.

John Traicos

Born: May 17, 1947, Zagazig, Egypt.
Height: 5ft 11¾in.   *Weight:* 11st 11lb.
Right-arm off-spin bowler.
Teams: South African Universities, Rhodesia, South Africa and Zimbabwe.

Career Highlights
1970: Played three Tests for South Africa *v* Australia, while still a university student.

John Traicos, who made his first class

debut in 1967 with the South African Universities team which toured England, took over the Zimbabwe captaincy in the 1983-84 season from Duncan Fletcher. Apart from being a very economical off-spinner, he is a stubborn late order batsman and a brilliant fielder, especially in the gully. He plays for Harare Sports Club. He was born in Egypt – of Greek parents.

Glenn Turner

Born: May 26, 1947, Dunedin, New Zealand.
Height: 5ft 9½in.   *Weight:* 11st 0lb.
Right-handed batsman.
Teams: Otago, Northern Districts, Worcestershire and New Zealand.

Career Highlights
1970: Set record for Worcestershire of 10 centuries in a season.
1972: Scored 672 runs for New Zealand in series in West Indies (at Georgetown he made 259, the highest Test score by a New Zealander, and his opening stand of 387 with Terry Jarvis is a record for the first wicket by New Zealanders in any first class match).
1973: First batsman for 35 years to complete 1,000 runs by end of May in an English season.
1974: Scored 101 and 110 not out at Christchurch to secure New Zealand's first-ever win over Australia.
1975-76: Held record aggregate for a New Zealand season (1,244).
1975: Amassed 333 runs (average 166.50) in World Cup.
1977: Set world record by scoring an unbeaten 141 in Worcestershire's total of 169 against Glamorgan, this being an unequalled 83 per cent of total.
1982: Completed the formidable feat

167

Glenn Turner

of 100 centuries in his first class career.

Glenn Turner is the plodder who became a plunderer. During his first season with Otago, he once scored only three runs in an entire morning session. And when he began playing county cricket for Worcestershire in 1968, he would play strictly within his limitations.

He was to mature into the complete batsman who crowned a marvellous career on May 29, 1982. He scored the century he wanted to complete his set of 100 hundreds – and he made the runs before lunch for Worcestershire against Warwickshire. He celebrated by calling for a gin and tonic, which he drank on the pitch, then he went on to score 311 not out in less than a day. It was a nice touch that the drink was served by Billy Ibadulla, the Pakistani who had remained on the Warwickshire staff after his playing days and who, on a coaching trip to Dunedin in the mid-sixties, had encouraged Turner to try his luck in England.

Such was Turner's determination that he gave up his office job for a better-paid night-shift in a bakery, to save the money to get to England. When he arrived, Warwickshire had their quota of overseas players ... which turned out to be Worcestershire's great gain. Of all the foreign players in the English game, nobody was more committed to his adopted county. Turner gave them 15 years' service.

His relationship with the New Zealand authorities has been less harmonious, although he reappeared for the Test team in 1983 after a break of six years initially caused by a disagreement over reimbursement of an air fare. He captained them in 10 Tests and was in at the start of their gradual emergence as a match for the other major Test-playing countries.

But it was to Worcestershire that he gave the greater part of his commitment and he was rewarded in 1978 with a £21,000 benefit.

Derek Underwood MBE

Born: June 8, 1945, Bromley, Kent, England.
Height: 5ft 11in.   *Weight:* 13st 0lb.
Slow left-arm bowler.
Teams: Kent and England.

Career Highlights
1963: Youngest bowler (18) to take 100 wickets in debut season.
1964: Kent's youngest player to be capped since Colin Cowdrey in 1951.
1967: Performed hat trick against Sussex at Hove.
1971: Match analysis of 12 for 97 against New Zealand at Christchurch included his 1,000th wicket in first class cricket. At 25 years and 264 days, he was third youngest player to achieve this – behind Wilfred Rhodes and George Lohmann.
1974: Returned best Test figures of eight for 51, including a spell of six for two, against Pakistan at Lord's.
1976-77: Took 29 wickets *v* India, to equal Fred Trueman's record in matches between the two countries set in 1952.
1981: Passed 2,000 career wickets.

The bowler colleagues and opponents call 'Deadly' celebrated 20 years in the first class game in 1983. Appropriately, he marked the anniversary by taking 106 wickets with his unique brand of slow-medium left-arm spin to put himself among the top 20 bowlers of all time. His total is 2,224. Of these, 297 have been claimed in Tests and had he not restricted his appearance in favour

Dilip Vengsarkar

of Kerry Packer and then been banned for going to South Africa he would have overtaken Fred Trueman's long-standing record for an Englishman of 307.

He played the first of his 86 Tests in 1966 at Nottingham and, although he finished wicketless against a powerful West Indies batting line-up, he demonstrated one of the attributes which was to sustain him over the years – the ability to keep it tight – bowling 45 overs for 91 runs. The following season he was back, against Pakistan, and this time a return of five for 52 steered England to a ten wickets victory.

Underwood is not renowned as a great spinner of the ball, but there has been no more accurate bowler in modern times. He possesses a subtle variation of pace, and he has been especially venomous in English conditions. When England beat the Australians at the Oval in 1968, a freak, lunch-time storm had turned the playing area into a lake. Volunteers helped ground staff mop up, but they weren't as effective as Deadly who got to work in the late afternoon with seven for 50, for a dramatic victory which halved the series.

Dilip Vengsarkar

Born: April 6, 1956, Bombay, India.
Height: 6ft 0in.   *Weight:* 11st 9lb.
Right-handed batsman.
Teams: Bombay and India.

Career Highlights
1979: Vengsarkar and Sunil Gavaskar hit an Indian record second wicket stand of 344 (unbroken) against West Indies in the New Year Test of 1979 at Calcutta.

Dilip Vengsarkar has established him-

self as India's No. 3 batsman in recent years, although he suffered the disappointment of missing out on their 1983 World Cup triumph, after being hit in the mouth by a delivery from West Indian Malcolm Marshall in a qualifying match.

He is an upright, correct player, who improved his best Test score when he made 159 in six and a half hours against the West Indies at Delhi in October 1983. He is the only Indian to hit two centuries at Lord's in Test matches.

Srinivas Venkataraghavan

Born: April 21, 1946, Madras, India.
Height: 5ft 11in.   *Weight:* 11st 12lb.
Right-arm off-spin bowler.
Teams: Tamil Nadu (formerly Madras), Derbyshire and India.

Career Highlights
1971: Took nine for 93 for Indians against Hampshire, at Bournemouth.

Venkat, as he is popularly abbreviated, was one of the famed India spinning quartet of the seventies with Chandrasekhar, Bedi and Prasanna. He began his Test career as an 18-year-old against New Zealand at Madras in 1965 and set up India's 1-0 win in the series by taking eight for 72 in the final Test at Delhi.

His popularity was such that there was a public outcry when he was dropped against Australia for the Bombay Test of 1969. His planned replacement, Bengal swing bowler Guha Subroto, agreed to withdraw and Venkat eventually played. Even then there was trouble, play carrying on despite a riot late on the fourth day, when Venkat was given out caught behind.

He captained India in two World Cups and led them in the 1979 series in England, when they fell only nine runs short of scoring 438 to win the final Test.

He was recalled to the Test attack in 1983 for the tour of West Indies, but his international career seemed over, when he was dropped again later in the year during the series against Pakistan. He had passed 150 Test wickets.

A likeable, modest cricketer, Venkat played three seasons with Derbyshire in the seventies.

Gundappa Viswanath

Born: February 12, 1949, Bhadravati, India.
Height: 5ft 4½in.   *Weight:* 10st 4lb.
Right-handed batsman.
Teams: Karnataka and India.

Career Highlights
1982: Highest score by an Indian in a Test match against England (222 at Madras).

When Gundappa Viswanath was dropped by India in 1983, a world record run of 87 Tests was ended. This dazzling little stroke-maker entered the international arena in 1969 at Kanpur against Australia. He hit 137 in his initial Test, thereby becoming the first person to score a century on both his Test and first class debuts. Two years previously he had announced himself with 230 for Mysore (now Karnataka) against Andhora.

'Vishy' is married to the sister of India's greatest batsman, Sunil Gavaskar, and although he has lacked brother-in-law's consistency there have been occasions when the brilliance of his attacking shots has overshadowed anything his teammates could produce.

His marathon 222 against England in 1982 lasted ten and a half hours and

Gundappa Viswanath

with two partners he helped put on 415 for the third wicket. Vengsarkar retired hurt after making 71, then Viswanath was joined by Yashpal Sharma, who hit 140.

Viswanath had passed 6,000 Test runs and made 14 centuries by the time he was dropped.

Bandula Warnapura

Bandula Warnapura

Born: March 1, 1953, Ceylon.
Height: 5ft 6in.   *Weight:* 9st 12lb.
Right-handed batsman.
Teams: Bloomfield and Sri Lanka.

Career Highlights
1982: Captained Sri Lanka in first ever Test match.

Bandula Warnapura captained Sri Lanka in their first ever Test match, against England in 1982. An opening batsman, he did not score heavily in four Tests before he was replaced for Sri Lanka's trip to Zimbabwe later that year. He then opted to join the rebel Sri Lankan tour to South Africa and was banned by his own country for 25 years.

Wasim Bari

Born: March 23, 1948, Karachi, Pakistan.
Height: 5ft 9in.   *Weight:* 12st 0lb.
Wicket-keeper and right-handed batsman.
Teams: Karachi, Sind, PIA and Pakistan.

Career Highlights
1977: Shared Pakistan's record 10th wicket stand of 133, set with Wasim Raja against West Indies at Bridgetown.
1979: Equalled record for most dismissals in a Test match innings, when he caught seven of first eight batsmen against New Zealand at Auckland.
1983: Passed 200 Test dismissals against India in Karachi.

Wasim Bari made his Test debut against England at Lord's as a 19-year-old in 1967 and has remained Pakistan's automatic choice wicket-keeper

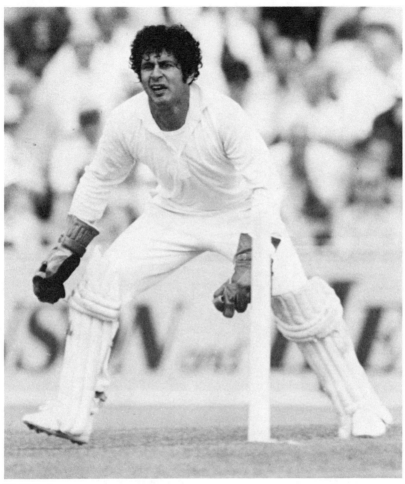

Wasim Bari

ever since. He is their most capped
player with 81 appearances following
the 1983-84 series against Australia,
and only Rodney Marsh and Alan
Knott have claimed more Test match
victims. He is the first 'keeper from his
country to achieve the double of 1,000
runs and 100 dismissals.

A determined late order batsman,
he captained Pakistan for six Tests.

Wasim Raja
Born: July 3, 1952, Multan, Pakistan.
Height: 5ft 9in.   *Weight:* 10st 2lb.
Left-handed batsman, right-arm leg-

Wasim Raja

spin bowler.

Teams: Lahore, Sargodha, Punjab
University, Camb. Universities, PIA,
Punjab, National Bank and Pakistan.

Career Highlights
1977: Hit 517 runs in series against
West Indies, and at Bridgetown set a
record 10th wicket stand for Pakistan
of 133 with Wasim Bari.
1983: Best Test score of 125 *v* India at
Jalandhar.

Raja is an all-rounder, who has rarely
given consistent evidence of his talent
in the Test arena, although he enjoyed
one golden series against West Indies
in 1977. Perhaps he has been
overawed by the dazzling array of batting skill which has usually preceded
him in the Pakistani order. He likes to
attack the bowling and hit 14 sixes in
the 1977 series against West Indies.
His leg-spin bowling has earned him
more than 500 wickets in first class
cricket since his debut as a 15-year-
old.

Dirk Wellham

Born: March 13, 1959, Marrickville,
New South Wales, Australia.
Height: 5ft 8½in.   *Weight:* 11st 5lb.
Right-handed batsman.
Teams: New South Wales and
Australia.

Career Highlights
1980: Scored 100 on his Sheffield
Shield debut for New South Wales
against Victoria at Melbourne.
1981: Completed an unusual double
when he made 103 on his Test debut
against England at the Oval.

Dirk Wellham, a bespectacled school
teacher, made a spectacular start to his
first class career in the 1980-81 Aus-

tralian season, scoring two centuries in
five matches and earning his place on
the tour to England which followed. He
topped Australia's averages, with 497
runs at 55.22, including a Test debut
century. But the following winter proved disastrous for him against the
West Indies pace bowlers.

However, he returned to form in
1982-83 with 1,205 runs, which helped
New South Wales to win the Sheffield
Shield, and he was appointed state
captain for 1983-84.

Kepler Wessels

Born: September 14, 1957,
Bloemfontein, South Africa.
Height: 6ft 1in.   *Weight:* 11st 7lb.
Left-handed batsman.
Teams: Orange Free State, Western
Province, Northern Transvaal,
Sussex, Queensland and Australia.

Career Highlights
1982: Scored 162 in his first Test
innings – against England at
Brisbane.

Kepler Wessels, a left-handed opening
batsman whose style is plain but very
effective, is one of the most consistent
players in the world. At 25 years old,
he had already passed 10,000 runs and
had a career average of just over 50.

He made his debut as a 16-year-old
in the South African Currie Cup competition and two years later joined Sussex, qualifying for Championship
matches in 1977. He played with them
for four seasons, with an interruption
for South African national service, and
in 1980 scored 1,800 runs, including
six centuries and a career best 254 *v*
Middlesex.

He was ambitious to play Test cricket, but preferred to try his luck with
Australia rather than England. He

Kepler Wessels

signed on with Queensland, where he found a great champion in Greg Chappell, and was given his chance at international level in 1982. His skill and temperament are ideally suited to the five day game, though he is far less happy in limited overs fixtures.

Sidath Wettimuny

Born: August 12, 1956, Colombo, Ceylon.
Height: 5ft 8in.   *Weight:* 9st 8lb.
Right-handed batsman, occasional seam bowler.
Teams: Sinhalese and Sri Lanka.

Career Highlights
1982: First batsman to score a Test century for Sri Lanka, with 157 against Pakistan at Faisalabad.

Sidath Wettimuny put himself in the record books with Sri Lanka's first Test century. And a year later, at Christchurch, he scored an unbeaten 63 to become the first player to carry his bat through a Test innings for Sri Lanka. He also opened the innings with his brother Mithra, to repeat the feat last recorded in 1880, when the Grace brothers, W. G. and E. M., opened for England at the Oval.

Mike Whitney

Born: February 24, 1959, Sydney, Australia.
Height: 6ft 0in.   *Weight:* 12st 9lb.
Left-arm fast medium bowler.
Teams: New South Wales, Gloucestershire and Australia.

Career Highlights
1981: Called up after six first class games to make his Test debut for Australia against England, playing in the final two matches of the series.

Mike Whitney, a qualified aircraft engineer, was plucked from obscurity when Australia were badly hit by injuries to their pace attack against England in 1981. The following winter he had a disappointing season back with New South Wales, picking up only nine wickets in six matches. However, in 1982-83, he helped his state win the Sheffield Shield with 45 wickets, including five for 95 against Victoria at Melbourne.

Peter Willey

Born: December 6, 1949, Sedgefield, County Durham, England.
Height: 6ft 1in.   *Weight:* 13st 0lb.
Right-handed batsman, off-spin bowler.
Teams: Northamptonshire, Eastern Province, Leicestershire and England.

Career Highlights
1971: Scored first century for England (100 not out) against West Indies at the Oval, when he also shared an unbroken last wicket stand of 117 with Bob Willis.
1976: Top score 65 in Northants' Gillette Cup final win over Lancashire at Lord's.
1982: Highest score of 186 for Northants *v* Yorkshire, Middlesbrough 1982.

Peter Willey is a combative batsman, who did as well as any of the England players in the torrid series against the fearsome pace attack of the West Indies in 1980 and the following winter. Infact, he averaged 48 in four Tests in the Caribbean. But the following summer he was dropped. *'When do we play the world champions again?'* he pointedly inquired of the England selectors. He joined the 1982 rebel tour to South Africa and is therefore banned from England consideration for three years.

He was only 16 when he first played for Northants. Strength in his forearms (he is said to be the only England cricketer to beat Ian Botham at arm wrestling) makes him a tremendously hard hitter of the ball without a great back lift and he is a fine player of fast bowling. However, he has sometimes been exposed by top class spinners. But he has improved with age.

He is also a passable off-spin bowler who took his career total of wickets beyond 500 in 1983.

Peter Willey

Bob Willis

Bob Willis MBE

Born: May 30, 1949, Sunderland, Tyne and Wear, England.
Height: 6ft 6in.   *Weight:* 14st 0lb.
Right-arm fast bowler.
Teams: Surrey, Warwickshire and England.

Career Highlights
1972: Hat trick for Warwickshire *v* Derbyshire.
1976: Another hat trick *v* West Indians.
1977: Took 100th Test wicket (*v* Australia) at Lord's. Best bowling for Warwickshire of eight for 32 against Gloucestershire at Bristol.
1980: Appointed county captain and led Warwickshire to Sunday League title.
1981: Achieved 100th Test wicket (*v* Australia at Nottingham). Took eight for 43 in England's sensational win at Leeds.

1983: Holds a quaint batting record –
first player to be not out 50 times in
Tests.

A great-hearted fast bowler, he took
over the England captaincy when
Keith Fletcher was sacked in 1982. His
career has several times been
threatened by knee injury, most
seriously in 1981 when he was forced
to return home early from England's
tour of the West Indies. But he
recovered to play a leading role that
summer in the winning of the Ashes.

Big Bob made his England debut in
January 1971, when, as an uncapped
Surrey player, he flew out to Australia
as a replacement. Twelve years later he
became the fourth bowler (and the
second Englishman, after Fred Trueman) to pass 300 wickets, reaching this
goal against New Zealand at Leeds.

Throughout most of his Test career,
Willis has carried the burden of being
England's main strike bowler, a responsibility he has accepted with single-
minded dedication.

He is not one of the game's great
tacticians, preferring to lead by personal example and demanding from his
players the maximum effort he himself
always contributes. Despite surrender-
ing the Ashes in 1982-83, he has led
England with dignity and is much respected by his fellow professionals.

He was christened Robert George,
but added the name Dylan at the age
of 12 because of his hero-worship of
the folk singer. His other heroes as a
teenager, when he played cricket in the
back garden with his brother, were
Brian Statham and John Snow. He was
to bowl alongside Snow on that first
trip to Australia.

Barry Wood

Born: December 26, 1942, Ossett,
Yorkshire, England.
Height: 5ft 7in.   *Weight:* 11st 0lb.
Right-handed batsman, right-arm
medium-paced bowler.
Teams: Yorkshire, Lancashire,
Derbyshire, Eastern Province and
England.

Career Highlights
1968: Best bowling 7 for 52 *v*
Middlesex at Manchester.
1972: Scored 90 on Test debut for
England *v* Australia at the Oval.
1976: Highest score for Lancashire of
198 *v* Glamorgan at Liverpool.
1981: Captained Derbyshire to victory
in the NatWest Trophy final against
Northants, Lord's.

Barry Wood is an opening batsman
and valued seam bowler (especially in
one-day matches), who made spas-
modic Test appearances while with
Lancashire between 1972 and 1979.

He was a vital member of Lancashire side which dominated English
limited overs cricket, winning Gillette
Cup four times in the seventies and
Sunday League in 1969 and 1970.

He joined Derbyshire in 1980,
enjoying a spell as their captain, and
was briefly recalled by England for the
one-day internationals against India in
1982. He left Derbyshire in 1983 and
had not found a county by early 1984.

Graeme Wood

Born: November 6, 1956, East
Freemantle, Western Australia,
Australia.
Height: 5ft 10in.   *Weight:* 12st 0lb.
Left-handed batsman.
Teams: Western Australia and
Australia.

Career Highlights
1980: Hit 112 in Centenary Test

Graeme Wood

against England at Lord's.

Graeme Wood has been a frequent, but inconsistent, opener for Australia since the Packer era. However, he was left out of the side again for the start of the 1983-84 series against Pakistan. Although he could boast seven Test centuries, he has had a fair share of failures. And his case has not been helped by his reputation as an erratic runner between the wickets.

Bob Woolmer

Born: May 14, 1948, Kanpur, India.
Height: 6ft 0in.   *Weight:* 13st 3lb.
Right-handed batsman, medium-
   paced bowler.
Teams: Kent, Natal, Western Province
   and England.

Career Highlights
1969: Best bowling 7 for 47 against
   Sussex at Canterbury.
1977: Hit two centuries in the series to
   help England win back the Ashes.
1982: Best score of 203 *v* Sussex at
   Tunbridge Wells.

If ever a Test career was surrendered it was Bob Woolmer's. He had established himself as England's number three batsman with scores of 120 and 137 in the first two Tests against Australia in 1977, then opted to sign for Kerry Packer. He was given chances to reclaim his place in 1980 and 1981, but could not reproduce his former fluency in the Test arena. He is now out in the cold again, being suspended for going to South Africa in 1982.

Woolmer made his debut for Kent as an all-rounder in 1968 and it was not until 1974 that he was given an opportunity as a batsman. He scored 1,000 runs for the first time the following season and spent several winters in

South Africa with Natal, where he was advised by Barry Richards.

England first used him as an all-rounder in 1975. But for his second Test he was moved up to number five and responded with 149 against Australia. He needed 394 minutes to reach his century – the slowest in matches between the two countries. But it helped England save a match after they had followed on.

Woolmer was born in India where his father was working in insurance. Dad had played as a batsman and off-spin bowler for Calcutta and placed a bat in baby Bob's cradle.

John Wright

John Wright

Born: July 5, 1954, Darfield, New
   Zealand.
Height: 6ft 1in.   *Weight:* 12st 6lb.
Left-handed batsman.
Teams: Northern Districts, Derbyshire
   and New Zealand.

Career Highlights
1982: Scored 141 *v* Australia, at
   Christchurch. That summer in
   England he totalled 1,830 runs for
   Derbyshire, including seven
   centuries. Two centuries in a match
   (113 and 105) Northern Districts *v*
   Auckland.
1983: Played in New Zealand's first
   Test match win in England, at Leeds.

John Wright made his debut in New
Zealand provincial cricket at the age of
20 and two years later sought a career
in England. He signed for Derbyshire
and he has since developed into a formidable opening batsman. At Napier
in 1979, he and Geoff Howarth set a
New Zealand second wicket record
with 195 against Pakistan. John, who
studied at Otago University, has a
degree in bio-chemistry.

Shivlal Yadav

Born: January 26, 1957, Hyderabad,
   India.
Height: 5ft 10in.   *Weight:* 11st 1lb.
Right-arm off-spin bowler.
Teams: Hyderabad and India.

Career Highlights
1979-80: Took 24 wickets in India's
   home series against Australia. He
   had a match return of seven for 81 in
   his Test debut at Bangalore.

Shivlal was recalled to India's Test
team against West Indies at Bombay in
1983, after a break of nearly two years.

In the previous Indian season, he had
improved his best bowling figures to
six for 49 for Hyderabad against
Kerala in a Ranji Trophy match at
Kothagudem.

Shivlal Yadav

Graham Yallop

Born: October 7, 1952, Balwyn,
   Melbourne, Australia.
Height: 6ft 0in.   *Weight:* 13st 0lb.
Left-handed batsman.
Teams: Victoria and Australia.

Career Highlights
1977: Two centuries in a match, 105
   and 114 not out, for Victoria *v* New
   South Wales at Sydney.
1978-79: Appointed captain of
   Australia *v* England.
1982-83: Set a Sheffield Shield record
   of 1,254 runs.

Graham Yallop was, perhaps, unlucky
to take on the Australia captaincy in

Graham Yallop (second left)

1978, when an inferior team, hard hit by defections to Kerry Packer, was out-manoeuvred by Mike Brearley's England. He partially redeemed his reputation as a leader by carrying off the Sheffield Shield for Victoria in successive seasons between 1978-80, although he resigned in 1983.

He has been an in and out member of the Australian batting line-up since the mid-seventies, though he has certainly had his moments of brilliance. He scored two good centuries in the 1978-79 Ashes series and was one of the few Aussies to emerge with any credit from the 1983 World Cup, topping their batting averages with 187 runs at 46.75.

Bruce Yardley

Born: September 5, 1947, Midland,
    Western Australia, Australia.
Height: 5ft 11in.   *Weight:* 12st 2lb.
Right-arm off-spin bowler, right-
    handed batsman.
Teams: Western Australia and
    Australia.

Career Highlights
1978: Seven for 44 for Western
    Australia *v* South Australia, at
    Adelaide.
1981-82: Australia's Cricketer of the
    Year.
1982: Took seven for 98 Australia *v*
    West Indies, at Sydney.

Bruce Yardley's career took a long time to get off the ground. He began life as an opening bowler and played for his state as a teenager. But competition was strong and he had to wait until he was 27, by which time he had switched to bowling off-spinners, before gaining a regular place. He got into the Test team during the Packer era, enjoying a successful tour of the

Bruce Yardley

West Indies in 1978 under Bobby Simpson. He was an irregular member of the side once Australia was back to full strength, but hit a high spot again in the early 1980's helping to win back the Ashes by taking 22 wickets against England in 1982.

Younis Ahmed

Born: October 20, 1947, Jullundur, India.
Height: 5ft 10in.   *Weight:* 11st 7lb.
Left-handed batsman, occasional left-arm spin or medium-paced bowler.
Teams: PIA, South Australia, Surrey,

Younis Ahmed

Worcestershire and Glamorgan.

Career Highlights
1969: Scored 1,760 runs for Surrey.
1979: Shared record fourth wicket
partnership for Worcestershire,
adding 281 with Alan Ormrod against
Nottinghamshire and going on to
make an unbeaten 221.

Younis appeared in first class cricket
in Pakistan at only 14 years old. His
brother Saeed Ahmed played 41 Tests,
but Younis has made just two
appearances for his country – against
New Zealand in 1969. He was later
banned by the Pakistan board for
coaching in Rhodesia (now Zimbabwe)
and South Africa. He was prolific during his early years with Surrey. He responded to a fresh challenge with
Worcestershire in 1979, making 1,539
runs. A powerful batsman with a wide
range of strokes, he became qualified
for England and was keen to play for
them, but his claims were ignored. He
was sacked by Worcestershire in 1983
for attempting to place a bet on them
to lose a Sunday League match. He
signed for Glamorgan for 1984.

Zaheer Abbas

Born: July 24, 1947, Sialkot, Pakistan.
Height: 5ft 11½in.   *Weight:* 11st 3lb.
Right-handed batsman.
Teams: Karachi, Sind, PIA,
Gloucestershire and Pakistan.

Career Highlights
1982: Became 20th player in game's
history to score 100 hundreds, when
he made 215 for Pakistan *v* India at
Lahore.

As a lad, Zaheer Abbas was advised by
his civil servant father not to take up
professional cricket. Fortunately for

the game's spectators, he ignored the
advice and went on to become one of
the great accumulators and at the same
time most attractive batsmen ever. He
has stated his philosophy clearly:
*'Scoring runs is my religion, after being
a Muslim. I have the same attitude as
Geoff Boycott.'* With Boycott, Zaheer
shares the distinction of having scored
his 100th hundred in a Test match.

Zaheer first gained attention when
Pakistan toured England in 1971. He
soon became conspicuous at the
crease, not only by his glinting gold-
rimmed spectacles. He scored 110 *v*
Worcestershire and was described by
Daily Express cricket writer, Crawford
White, as the most impressive new-
comer to England since Bradman 41
years previously! Such a comparison
did not seem far fetched when Zaheer
hit 274 in the first Test at Edgbaston.
His 291 stand with Mushtaq Mohammad was a second wicket record for
Pakistan against allcomers. He was
offered a contract by Gloucestershire
and has been demolishing records ever
since.

In 1976, he scored 2,554 runs in the
English season, the highest total since
the reduction of Championship
matches in 1969. Back home in 1973-
74 he had established a record for the
Pakistani season with 1,597.

He has four times scored unbeaten
double centuries in the same match.
And in 1981, after a wet start to the
season prevented him having an innings in April or May, he scored 1,016
runs in June.

Zaheer passed 4,000 runs in Tests
during the series against India, 1982-
83, and has been battling with Javed
Miandad for the position of Pakistan's
leading run-getter of all time. However,
Javed's age advantage means that this
is one contest Zaheer is likely eventually to lose.

Zaheer Abbas

Acknowledgements

Data compiled by **Peter Tozer**, who acknowledges assistance from Bill Frindall, D. J. Rutnagur, Ted Morley, Rob Batsford, S. S. Perera and K. N. Prabhu and Sports Media Services, Sydney.